THE HARMONY GUIDE TO

DRESS MAKING

Lyric Books Limited

© 1991 Lyric Books Limited
PO Box 152, Mill Hill, London NW7, England

First Published in 1991

ISBN 0 07111 0072 1

Printed in Belgium by
Proost International Book Production

Compiled by Stefanie Paradine and
Felicity Murray in association with Simplicity

Edited by Debra Mountford

Series Editor Beryl Kempner

Contents

Introduction

Dear Reader,

Welcome to the Harmony Guide to Dressmaking.

This book has been written for dressmakers of all levels. Total beginners will find step-by-step instructions enabling them to work their first project with care and confidence - experienced dressmakers will find tips on quick and easy alternatives to some of the traditional methods where these are advantageous.

The Harmony Guides are all intended to enhance your enjoyment of their particular subject and we hope you will find that the Guide to Dressmaking does just that. Enjoy your sewing.

Beryl Kempner

Beryl Kempner

Series Editor

I. Tools

Everything You Need to Get Started

A meander around a good haberdashery store can be quite inspiring. There is a wealth of fascinating notions to help you create your own fashions. You will find everything imaginable, from accessories like ribbons and bows, sequinned motifs, feathers, buttons, popper fastenings and every style of zip fastener, to the basic essentials. Listed here are some of the basic tools of the trade to help make your sewing as fast, easy and enjoyable as possible.

Bent Handle Shears

Dressmakers shears have angled handles to allow the blades to rest on the table as you cut out your fabric. Choose a pair with a comfortable handle that accommodates all your fingers and is not stiff to open and close. The blades should be 18 cm or 21 cm (7" or 8") long. Invest in a good pair and they will serve you well if you look after them - do not use them for cutting paper or anything other than fabric and pattern tissue.

Small Sharp Scissors

These are for snipping threads, clipping into seam allowances and detail work. They should have 7 to 10 cm (3" to 4") pointed blades.

Pinking Shears

These are an optional extra. They are used to neaten the raw edges of the fabric but are not so necessary if you have a sewing machine which over sews raw edges.

Tape Measure

Choose one that is at least 150 cm (60") long with metal tipped ends and clearly marked measurements on both sides. The best are plastic coated which will not stretch or tear.

Yard Stick

This is an invaluable measuring aid, made in metal or wood. It is also available in metre lengths.

Ruler

Plastic see-through ones are particularly useful.

Pins and Needles

There are many different types of sewing needle, the one you choose depends on the task at hand. For general sewing medium length 'sharps' are most often used. They are suitable for most weights of fabric. For knitted fabric use 'ball-point' needles, their rounded point slips between the fibres, rather than splitting them as you sew.

Machine needles also are available in a range of sizes and with different types of points. Sharp pointed needles are used for woven fabrics, ball points for knits and wedge shape points for leathers.

Pins should be rustproof stainless steel. Use finer pins for easily marked very fine fabrics. Pins with coloured heads are easy to see and excellent for general dressmaking.

Needle Threader

This handy little device can sometimes save both time and temper.

Thimble

Not essential for most sewing tasks but there will be times when the sewing gets tough that you will be glad you bought one.

Pin Cushion

A useful accessory for safely keeping needles and pins to hand.

An Un-picker or Seam Ripper

This often comes as an accessory with the sewing machine. It is a simple pen-like device that allows quick and accurate cutting of threads down a seam between the two layers of fabric. Care must be taken to avoid cutting the fabric accidentally.

Tailors Chalk, Tracing Wheel and Tracing Paper

These are used to transfer pattern markings on to the fabric. The chalk - handiest in the form of a dressmakers pencil and sharpener, is useful when marking hemlines etc. The tracing wheel and paper are used to mark the positions of darts, pleats, pockets, buttons etc. The carbon-like paper is inserted between the layers of fabric, and the tracing wheel is used to transfer the pattern markings, also see pages 21 and 22.

Iron

Ideally this should be the best you can afford, fast heating with a good heavy steam facility, water spray, and easily controllable temperature.

Ironing Board

This should be sturdy, level and evenly padded. Keep the cover clean and smooth. A sleeve board is useful for pressing sleeves and collars. Also keep at hand a pressing cloth (a linen tea-towel is ideal) and brown paper for placing under folds of darts or seam turnings to prevent unsightly ridges appearing on the right side as you press.

Sewing Machine

This is a very personal choice dependent upon your pocket as much as anything. A basic machine with a swing-needle action will tackle almost every dressmaking task. Ask yourself how often you are likely to use all the other facilities on a highly sophisticated computerised version - does this justify its cost? Remember a machine is only as good as its operator!

Overlocker

Traditionally this is an industrial machine that stitches, trims and overcasts all in one operation. Every devoted dressmaker's dream machine - but only for the experienced and dedicated - this would be a costly and unnecessary luxury for a beginner or occasional user.

Cutting Surface

You will need a large firm flat surface preferably at least 1 m x 2 m (36" x 72") and accessible from all sides. The dining room table will be less backbreaking than the floor.

Sewing Thread

It is as important to use the right type of thread as it is to colour match your chosen fabric. There are many different threads, including specialist threads, which you use depends on your fabric choice and stitching requirements, (see page 20).

The Simple Way to a Perfect Fit

One of the great advantages of making your own clothes is being able get a perfect fit. Finding a pattern to fit your body shape is much easier than you may think, and simple alterations can be made to perfect that fit. Today's patterns are clearly marked with guide lines for lengthening and shortening, and with multi-size patterns it is possible to cut your top a size smaller or larger than the bottom simply by following the relevant cutting out lines.

But first and most importantly, you need to find your pattern size. Do not just presume you know your size, your pattern size may not correspond with your ready-to-wear size. Garment manufacturers all have their own sets of standard measurements (which is why you can find you are a size 14 in one shop and a 12 or 16 in another). Fortunately with paper patterns the sizing is far more reliable because you are given, for every size, the exact measurements that the finished garment is designed to fit. Any fashion fullness (or tightness) will have been allowed for, leaving you simply to match the nearest pattern size to your own.

It is therefore most important to measure yourself (carefully and **honestly**). Then, by comparing your measurements with those given for the different figure types, you can decide which type you are, and select your size from within that type.

Time spent checking your size at this stage ensures you find the best fitting pattern for your body shape and ultimately gives a much more satisfying end result.

Taking Your Measurements

The surest way of knowing your figure, and selecting the right pattern to fit, is by taking all the measurements indicated in these figure illustrations. Make a list of them and then compare them directly with those given on your pattern.

Use these tips to help you take measurements correctly.

1. Do not attempt to measure yourself - enlist the help of a friend.

2. Take the measurements over your usual underwear.

3. Try and stand in a relaxed, normal way (but not slouched), looking straight ahead.

4. Tie a piece of string around your waist as a guide line. If you have problems finding the natural waistline, bend sideways - the crease that forms is the waistline.

5. To find the shoulder point raise the arm to shoulder height and the dimple that forms marks the spot!

6. The back (nape) of the neck can be found by bending the head forward so that you can feel the first prominent neck bone or vertebra.

7. When taking the chest and hip measurements keep the tape level, parallel to the ground, and snug to the body, but not too tight.

Your height and back to waist length will help initially to determine your basic figure type, and your bust (or chest), waist and hips will decide on the size within that figure type. Other measurements are used if fine-tuning on the pattern itself is necessary. But it is only possible to check a pattern for its fit if you do have all these measurements at hand.

What to Measure

1. **Height** total height without shoes.

2. **Back Neck to Waist Length** from prominent bone at neck base to waist.

3. **Neck** (men) measure at the Adam's apple, add 1.5 cm ($\frac{1}{2}$").

4. **High Bust** (women) under the arms, above the bust and across the widest part of the back.

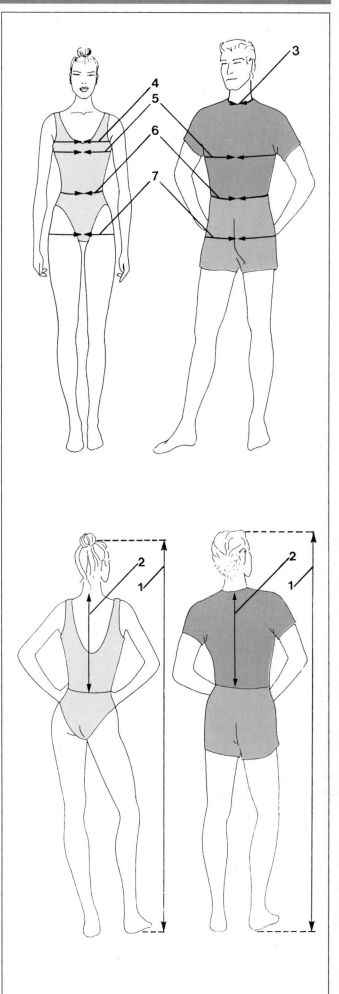

II. Sizes

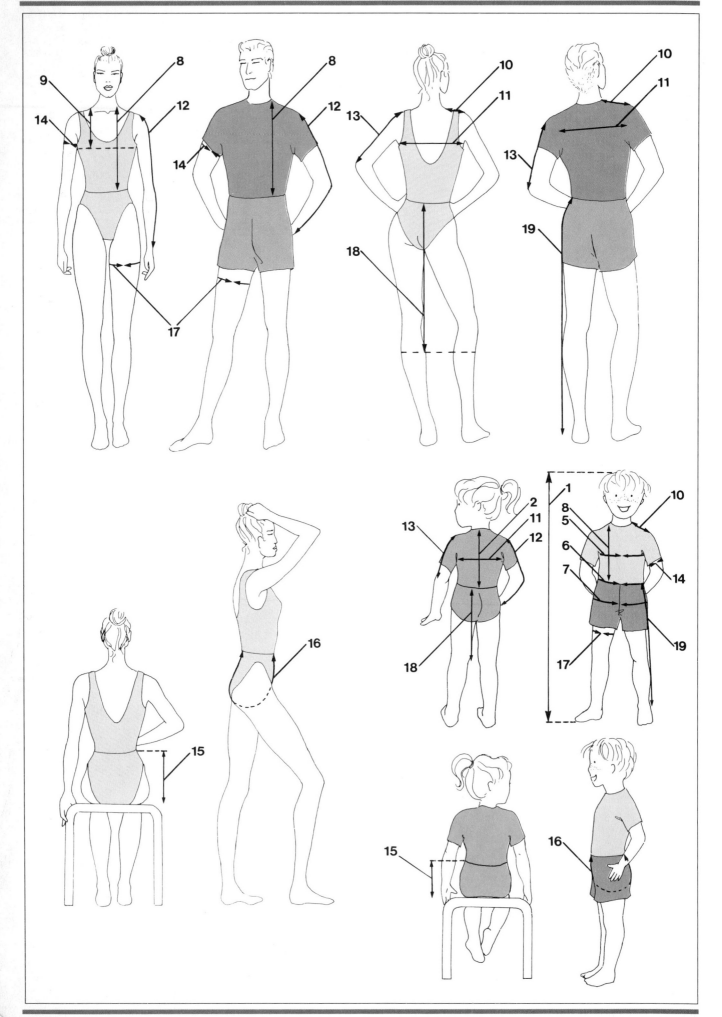

5. Bust/chest over the fullest part, keeping the tape straight across the back.

6. Waist (see note 4 in Taking Your Measurements on page 7).

7. Hips around the fullest part, approximately 18 to 23 cm (7" to 9") below the waist.

8. Front Neck to Waist Length from the shoulder at the neck base to the front waist (over the bust/chest).

9. Shoulder to Bust Point from shoulder at neck base to bust point.

10. Shoulder Length from neck base to shoulder point (see note 5 in Taking Your Measurements on page 7).

11. Back Width across the mid back.

12. Arm Length from shoulder bone to wrist bone over a slightly bent elbow.

13. Shoulder to Elbow from shoulder bone to mid elbow.

14. Upper Arm around fullest part.

15. Crotch Depth, sit on a hard chair and measure from side waist to chair seat.

16. Crotch Length from centre back waist, between legs to centre front waist.

17. Thigh around the fullest part.

Non-essential but handy-to-have measurements

18. Skirt Length from centre back waist to desired length.

19. Trouser Length from side waist to desired length.

To determine your figure type, compare your bust, waist, hip and height measurements with those of the figure types in pattern books to see which corresponds with your own body configurations. They will probably not correspond exactly with any one size but try to find the closest. Height is one indicator of figure type - and the length of your back in relation to your bust, waist and hips is important to determine body proportion.

Having determined your figure type you can now list the closest measurements next to your own for a final analysis.

If you are uncertain because your size above the waist differs from your size below your waist, consider also which size would be best suited for the design you have chosen. If you are making a skirt the waist and hip measurements are the deciding factor, and likewise if you are making a blouse only the bust and upper torso measurements need be considered. Multi-size patterns are ideal for this figure type as it is possible to combine pattern pieces of two different sizes.

The Pattern Envelope

The pattern envelope has all the information you need to know about a pattern before you start sewing. The picture on the front will help in your pattern selection and the back of the envelope will help you to select your fabric and notions. It will also give you additional information, including back views, and any details that are not shown in the illustration. Read these carefully to be sure you are buying exactly the style you want. Now check the rest of the information given.

Body Measurements

Do you have your right size? Body measurements are given for the size or sizes included in the envelope - are they yours? See Taking Your Measurements on page 7.

Fabric Requirements

Meterages (yardages) are given for every garment or version (sometimes indicated by a number or letter referring to an illustrated view on the envelope front). Also for any additional fabrics required (for linings, interfacings or trims for example). Sizes are given across the top and fabric widths down the side. Fabric widths will have nap indications beside them. Check whether the allowance given is for fabric with or without a nap

or one-way design.

Fabrics with a nap (or directional fabrics) have cutting out layouts with all the pieces laid in one direction and therefore normally require more fabric.

Garment Measurements

These give you vital additional information about the fit. For example, the finished skirt, jacket or trouser lengths plus the widths at the hems. From these you can see whether you will need to lengthen, shorten or alter any pieces of the pattern, (see Adjusting the Fit on page 10).

Garment Description

This explains details not obvious on the illustration, like lining, top-stitching and pockets, plus design variations on each view.

Fabric Selection

This information is important and will tell you if the pattern is suitable for fabrics with a nap or strong directional pattern. Or if it is suitable for a particular type of fabric only - such as knitted.

The list of suggested suitable fabrics is for well known fabric types which you can use as a general guideline. The key points are weight and handle - whether the fabric should be soft, to drape; or crisp, to hold a shape.

Notions

This is a list of specific accessories that will be required to make the garment. For example, the size and quantity of buttons, the zip length, hooks and eyes, seam binding, etc.

Typical Pattern Information
Ladies mid-calf length dress with gathered skirt into fitted, shaped bodice, with neckline and sleeve variations.
Suggested fabrics - Cotton types, chambray, lawn. No allowance made for matching plaids, checks, stripes or large patterned fabrics.
Notions - 55 cm (22") zip, hooks and eyes.

	SIZE	8	10	12	14	16	18	
Metric	Bust	80	83	88	92	96	100	cm
	Waist	64	66	70	74	78	82	cm
	Hip	88	90	94	98	102	106	cm
Fabric requirements								
Views 1, 3	115 cm*	4.90	4.90	5.00	5.00	5.10	5.10	m
	150 cm*	3.50	3.60	3.80	3.90	3.90	3.90	m
Views 2, 4	115 cm*	4.80	4.80	4.80	4.90	4.90	4.90	m
	150 cm*	3.70	3.70	3.70	3.70	3.80	3.90	m
Garment measurements								
Length from base of neck		115	115	116	116	118	118	cm
Width at lower edge		269	269	282	282	292	292	cm
Inches	Bust	31½	32½	34	36	38	40	ins
	Waist	24	25	26½	28	30	32	ins
	Hip	33½	34½	36	38	40	42	ins
Fabric requirements								
Views 1, 3	45 ins*	5⅜	5⅜	5½	5½	5⅝	5⅝	yd
	60 ins*	3⅞	4	4¼	4⅜	4⅜	4⅜	yd
Views 2, 4	45 ins*	5¼	5¼	5¼	5⅜	5⅜	5⅜	yd
	60 ins*	4⅛	4⅛	4⅛	4⅛	4¼	4⅜	yd
Garment measurements								
Length from base of neck		45¼	45¼	45¾	45¾	46½	46½	ins
Width at lower edge		106	106	111	111	115	115	ins

* fabric without nap, ** with nap, *** with or without nap

Instruction Sheet

The instruction sheet inside the pattern envelope will gives all the step by step instructions required to make up your garment. But first it is important to understand the general terminology.

III. Adjusting the Fit

Fine-tuning the Fit

This is where all the the extra measurements you have taken come into play. Having chosen your style and bought a pattern in the nearest size to your own, you can now do a little fine-tuning if necessary, to perfect the fit.

An important factor to take into account before altering a pattern is the amount of 'ease' that will have been allowed. The pattern piece will measure more than your body because otherwise the garment would be skin tight (although with some designs this may be close to the requirement). So do not be tempted to measure the pattern pieces as a guide to fit because this could be misleading, except perhaps in the case of the length of a skirt or trouser leg. The crotch seam is the only true exception to this rule - this **must** be measured on the pattern and compared directly with your body measurement to be sure of a perfect fit, (see Fitting Trousers on page 14).

Apart from the trouser crotch, patterns should be adjusted to fit by comparing your measurements to those listed on the pattern envelope.

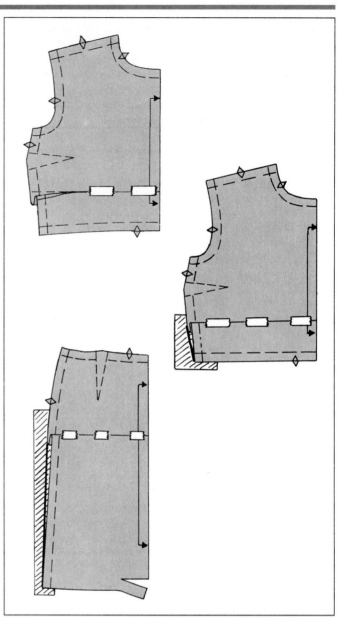

To Alter or Not to Alter

Do not be tempted to over-fit. If the difference between your body measurement and the pattern envelope measurements is 1.5 cm (1/2") or less around the bust, waist or hips, it will not be worth altering the pattern. This adjustment can be made by taking a fractionally narrower or greater seam allowance.

Likewise, if the difference is 5 mm (1/4") or less around the crotch or in the bodice length, it is not worth worrying about. However, if the difference is anything more, it will be worth spending a few minutes making adjustments.

Having Decided to Alter

Having made the decision to alter a pattern be sure you make the same adjustments to all corresponding pattern pieces. For example, if you have adjusted the overall measurement of the front bodice, be sure to adjust the back bodice piece as well or your side seams will not match. Or, if you have adjusted the waist size of a skirt by adding or subtracting from the side seams or darts, remember to adjust the waistband by the corresponding amount.

When you are adding to a pattern you will need to pin or tape extra paper underneath. If you are subtracting from a pattern, try to make tucks or folds where possible, rather than cutting, in case you want to let it out again at a later date.

Note: For any adjustments it is advisable to test the fit of these changes by constructing the section in muslin or off-cuts of any fabric of a similar weight and texture to the one you will be using.

Adjusting for Length

In many cases printed lines on the pattern piece indicate where to lengthen or shorten. Sometimes you can also change the length at the lower edge, depending on the garment style.

To shorten

Measure up from the printed lengthen/shorten line the amount by which you need to shorten the piece. Draw another line parallel to the original one at this point.

Bring the two lines together making a tuck in the pattern. Fold along the printed line. Pin or tape the fold in place. Re-draw the cutting lines if necessary.

At the lower edge measure and mark the change then cut, or preferably fold under, the excess pattern paper (you may wish to lengthen it at a later date).

To lengthen

Cut along the printed shorten/lengthen line. Pin or tape the cut edge of the upper section to a strip of paper.

Measure down from the cut edge the amount by which you

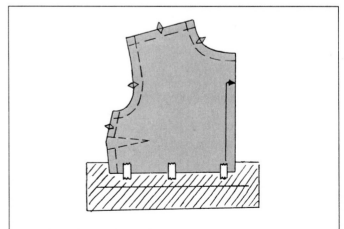

need to lengthen the pattern and draw a line parallel to the edge.

Align the cut edge of the lower section to the drawn line and pin or tape in place.

With ruler and pencil join up the cutting and sewing lines at the side edges.

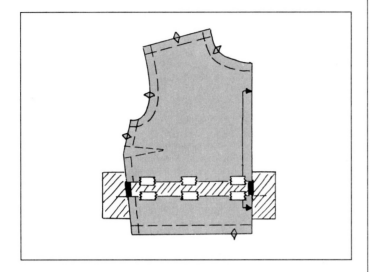

At the lower edge add a strip of paper the to hem edge then extend the cutting lines and re-draw the lower edge (checking with a ruler that you have an added an equal amount right across the pattern).

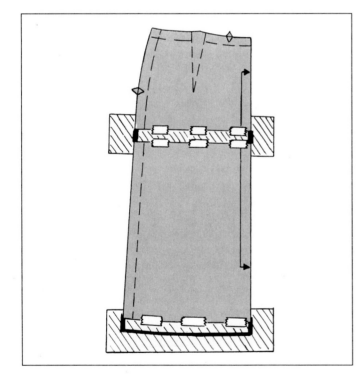

Adjusting for Width

Note: If you need to adjust more than a total of 5 cm (2") on a hip or waist measurement, you should check your pattern size. You may need to buy a larger or smaller size.

Hips

Add or subtract a quarter of the total amount (5 cm (2") or less) at the sides of the front and back pieces (down entire length of the seam, tapering to the printed cutting line just below the waist).

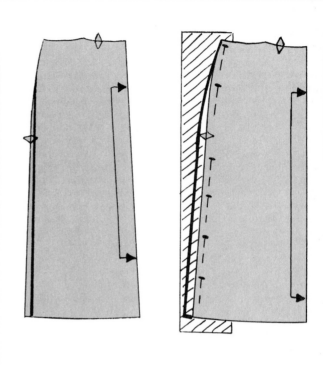

Adjusting for extra large hips

If you are having to increase the hip measurement by more than 5 cm (2") slash the front and back pattern pieces through the dart points to the lower edge, parallel to the centre back line or straight grain. Insert a strip of paper one quarter of the total amount to be added. Reduce the waist to its original measurement by increasing the top width of the dart, and tapering the side seam above the hip.

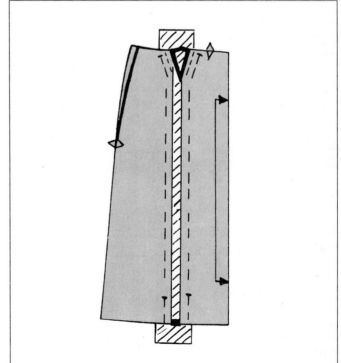

III. Adjusting the Fit

Waist

Add or subtract a quarter of the total amount at the waist edge of the side seams (on each side of both the front and back pattern pieces).

Taper the new cutting line to meet the printed cutting line above the hip. Now adjust the waistband by the corresponding amount at the marks which indicate the side seam positions.

If the pattern pieces have darts at the waist on the front and back, add or subtract an eighth of the total amount to this, then re-taper the dart. Only an eighth of the total amount then has to be added or subtracted to the side as previously described.

Bust Adjustments

To increase or decrease up to 2.5 cm (1")

Mark half of the amount of increase or decrease at the side seam along the bustline. (For an increase place extra paper under the side edges).

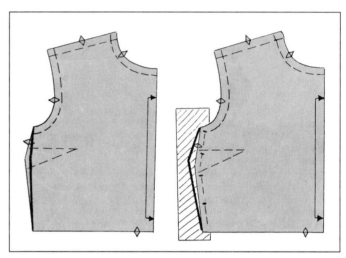

Draw a new cutting line, tapering up to the original line at the armhole and down to the original line at the waistline, extending ends of dart if necessary.

To increase or decrease more than 2.5 cm (1")

The requirement for this amount of adjustment indicates that you are larger or smaller than the average cup size the pattern was designed for. Since adding or subtracting 2.5 cm (1") or more from the side seams will distort the fit of the garment, some other remedies are required.

First Locate the Bust Point on Your Pattern

If your pattern has both horizontal and vertical bust darts, extend a line through the centre of each dart, mark where they intercept and that is the bust point.

If your pattern does not have both horizontal and vertical darts:

1. Subtract your shoulder to bust measurement from your front waist length measurement. Measure up that distance from the waistline and make a mark.

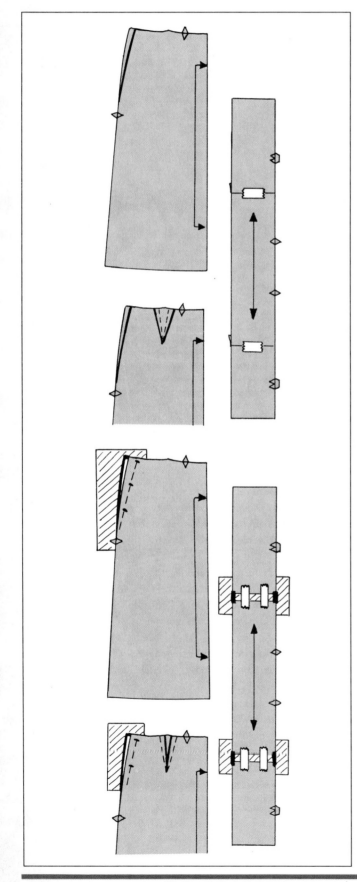

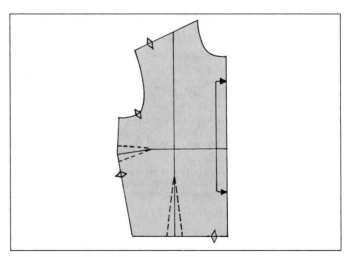

2. Draw a horizontal line that intercepts the mark at a right angle to the grainline or centre front line.

3. Draw a vertical line, parallel to the grainline or centre front line, from the mid point of the shoulder to the waistline. The point of intersection indicates the bust point.

To increase the cup size

1. Place a piece of paper under the pattern keeping the centre front aligned, slash the pattern along the horizontal line and spread it apart by the amount needed for the front neck to waist length adjustment. Pin or tape in place.

2. Slash along the vertical line, just to, but not through, the cutting lines at the shoulder seam and waistline or hemline.

3. Keeping the grainline or centre front line straight, spread the vertical cut edges a quarter of the amount needed for the bust adjustment, tapering to nothing at the shoulder seam and waistline. Pin or tape the cut edges in place.

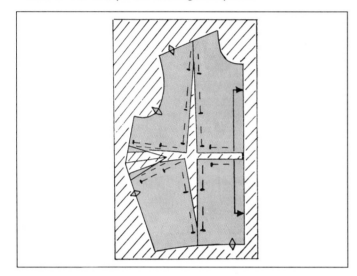

Because you have lengthened the garment in the bust area (where you need it) you have also lengthened it at the side seam (where you do not). You will therefore have to add or re-draw the side seam bust dart as shown. This will take up the extra length at the side.

To decrease the cup size

Reverse the steps for increasing the cup size, overlapping the pattern instead of spreading it. This time because you have shortened the garment in the bust area (where you need it) and at the side seam (where you do not) you will have to re-draw the existing dart or add the necessary length to the lower edge of the garment at the side seam.

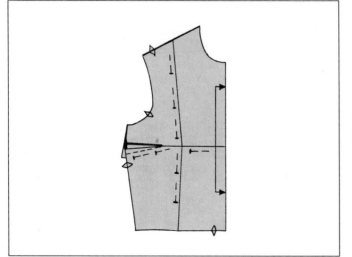

Shoulder Length

To adjust up to 5 mm (1/4")

Mark the amount inside (to shorten) or outside (to lengthen) the shoulder seam at the armhole. Draw a new cutting line tapering to the original line at the armhole notch. Do this on both the front and back pattern pieces.

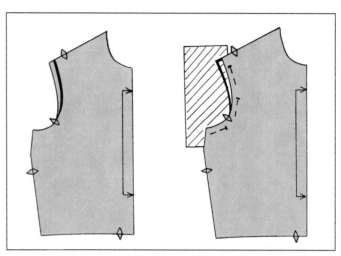

Because this adjustment may affect the way the sleeve hangs on the finished garment, tack/baste the sleeve in place first and try on the garment before stitching. If necessary, pull out the tacking/basting stitches and re-position the sleeve until it hangs properly, then stitch in place. Adjustments of more than 5 mm (1/4") are not recommended unless a balancing adjustment is made to the sleeve head, which could require re-drawing the sleeve top completely.

Back Width

To adjust up to 2.5 cm (1")

Draw a horizontal line at right angles to the centre back or grainline through the base of the armhole at the side seam. Draw a vertical line, parallel to the grainline or centre back line, from the mid point of the shoulder to the waistline. Slash along the line from the side seam to the intersection point and then to the shoulder, do not cut through the seam.

To decrease back width

Over lap the edges of the slash at intersection point, by the required amount. Pin or tape the edges in position. Re-draw the shoulder line and the side seam from the base of armhole.

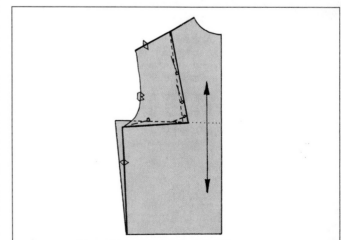

III. Adjusting the Fit

To increase back width

Spread the slash at intersection point, by the required amount. Pin or tape the edges in position. Re-draw the shoulder line and the side seam from the base of armhole.

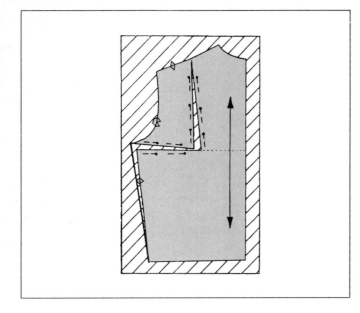

Because this adjustment may affect the way the sleeve hangs on the finished garment, tack/baste the sleeve in place first and try on the garment before stitching. If necessary, pull out the tacking/basting stitches and re-position the sleeve until it hangs properly, then stitch it in place. Adjustments of more than 2.5 cm (1") are not recommended unless a balancing adjustment is made to the sleeve which could mean re-drawing it completely.

Fitting Trousers

Trousers need to fit well for both comfort and style. For a good fit getting the crotch measurement right is essential.

There is no standard crotch length or depth in the chart. This is the one time that you **must** check your own measurements against the actual pattern pieces.

Crotch Depth

Check and adjust the crotch depth **before** checking or adjusting the crotch length.

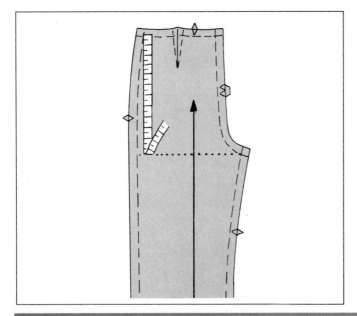

First measure from the crotch line on the pattern up to the waistline seam. Take your measurement line close to the side seam, but parallel to the grainline. This measurement should be equal to your crotch depth, (see Taking Your Measurements on page 7) plus approximately 1.5 cm (1/2") of ease for hips up to 90 cm (36") and up to 3 cm (11/4") ease for larger hips.

Use the lengthen/shorten line on the pattern to adjust if required, (see Adjusting for Length on page 10).

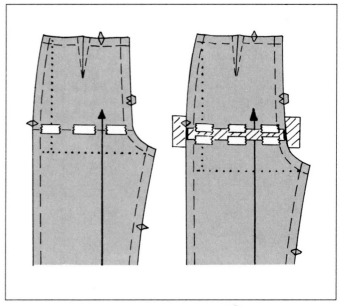

Crotch Length

Measure along the stitching line of both centre front and centre back seams (the crotch seam) from the waist seamline to the inner leg seamline. Add these two measurements together. This crotch measurement should be equal to your crotch measurement **plus** 3.5 to 5 cm (11/2" to 2") ease allowance (without which you will not be able to sit down comfortably!).

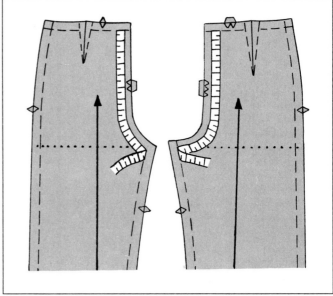

Exactly how you make this adjustment depends partly on your own shape. You can simply add or subtract an equal amount on both pattern pieces or if, for example, you have a large bottom and a flattish stomach, you could add more to the back than the front.

Shorten or lengthen the crotch by subtracting or adding half (or as required) the adjustment amount at the inner leg seams as shown, tapering to the notch on the cutting line further down the leg.

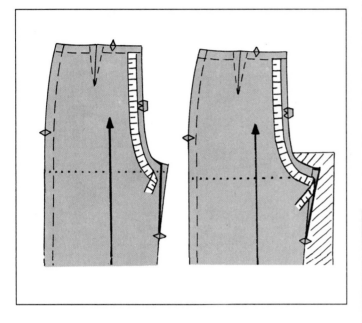

Fit as You Sew

After you have stitched the basic construction seams, try the garment on over the appropriate undergarments. Any further fine-tuning can be done now without too much trouble. Where a precise fit is required it is advisable to tack/baste these key seams first before stitching. Shoulder pads can make a tremendous difference to the hang and fit of a garment and solve many a problem - so do have a few pads of various sizes and thicknesses available for fitting sessions.

On your final fitting you should check the length before hemming - some fabrics can drop and affect your hemline.

Fabric Terminology

Woven Fabrics

The **selvedges** are the finished edges along either side of the fabric length. Unlike the cut crosswise edges these will not fray. The **grain** is the direction in which the threads making up the fabric run. All woven fabrics have warp and weft (lengthwise and crosswise) threads. The threads running parallel to the selvedge (warp threads) indicate the **lengthwise** or **straight grain**. The threads running across the fabric from selvedge to selvedge (weft threads) indicate the **crosswise grain**.

The **true bias** is at an angle of 45 degrees to the selvedges, and on this line the fabric has maximum give or stretchiness. This is used to advantage particularly on curved pattern pieces, such as collars or circular skirts.

The grainlines are indicated on the pattern pieces and the cutting layout, with arrows.

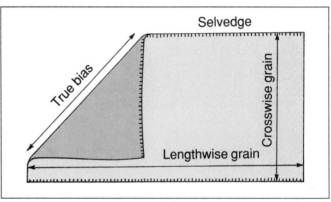

Knit Fabrics

Knitted fabrics are made up of interlocking loops of yarn. **Wales** or ribs are columns of loops running the length of the fabric. **Courses** are the crosswise rows of loops. Knitted fabrics are made flat or tubular. Tubular fabrics can be cut open along one edge following a lengthwise column of rib loops.

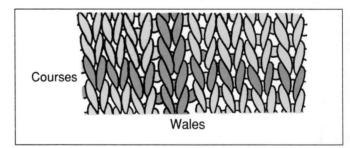

Choosing the Right Fabric

When choosing a fabric first refer to the recommended fabric types listed on the envelope back. Check whether the pattern is suitable for the type of fabric you have in mind. Some patterns are not suitable for one-way designs or fabrics with a nap (pile). Think about the scale of the fabric design also - is a bold design going to work? For example, if the pattern has many seams which are going to break up the design, a smaller all-over repeat may be a better choice.

Preparing Your Fabric

Before you begin to position the pattern pieces, it is important

IV. Fabrics

to lay out the fabric correctly. First iron out any creases or folds in the direction of the lengthwise or crosswise grain only and **not** on the bias diagonal, taking care not to stretch the fabric. Now you can fold the fabric length (usually with right sides together) as indicated in the relevant diagram for your size, fabric width and type. Fabrics with a one-way design or pile (such as velvet or corduroy) will have their own layout because these require all the pattern pieces to be laid in one direction.

Make sure that the fabric is laying true and that there are no puckers. If you have a bold print like a stripe or plaid, ensure that the under layer is aligned with the upper layer. If the fabric grain is not true to start with your pattern pieces will not be cut on the correct grain and your finished garment will not hang well.

Matching up a bold print requires a little skill, (see Fabrics that Require Special Handling on page 17). Therefore any pattern which is dependent on a good match at the seams requires extra care when placing the pattern pieces.

To 'true' the fabric, start by straightening the ends. With a woven fabric the best way is to snip into the selvedge and pull a crosswise thread until the fabric puckers. Then cut along that puckered line. Tearing the fabric is the quickest means, but care should be taken as the tugging can pull the fabric off grain for a few inches, or the fabric may suddenly split and tear lengthwise. Of course if the fabric has a distinct design which is woven in and not printed on, you can use this as a guide for cutting a straight line across the fabric width.

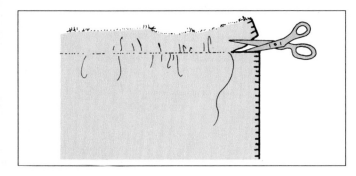

For a knitted fabric, cut along a course (crosswise row) of loops.

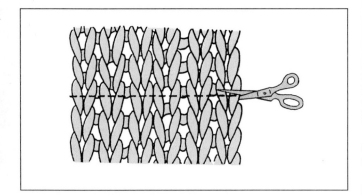

Next identify which is the right and wrong side of the fabric - this is not always obvious. As a general rule, cottons are folded on the bolt with right side out and wools, or delicate fabrics, right side inwards. The wrong side of a selvedge will look less finished in appearance and, with knitted fabrics, the cut edge will tend to roll towards the right side when pulled.

The Cutting Layout

On the first page of your instruction sheet will be a variety of cutting diagrams or cutting layouts. It is helpful to circle the layout that you are to follow.

Identify

1. Which pieces you need for the pattern view and size you are making and remove them from the envelope.

2. Which diagram relates to your fabric width (and pattern size). If you are using a fabric with a one-way design or nap there may be an alternative layout to allow for this.

3. The shadings on the diagrams. There will be a key on the sheet to help you identify the right and wrong side of the fabric, pattern pieces and interfacings.

Folding the Fabric

A lengthwise fold is when the fabric is folded in half along its length with selvedges matching at one side. This fold is used for plain or uncomplicated fabrics without a nap or one-way design.

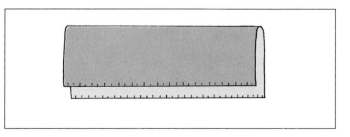

A crosswise fold is when the fabric is folded across its width, selvedges matching on both sides. This fold is also used for fabrics without a nap or one-way design, but is only recommended where a particular design placing is not required.

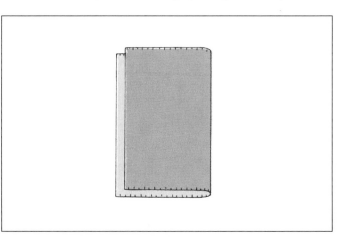

Single thickness is when one layer of fabric is placed right side up. It is used for fabrics with a nap or one-way design.

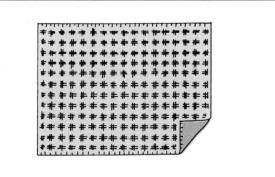

A crosswise cut is used for fabrics that have a nap or one-way design. The fabric is folded in half along the crosswise grain, then cut along the fold. The top layer is then turned around so that the nap is running in the same direction on both layers.

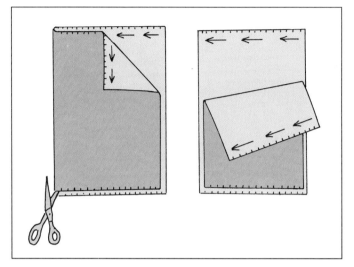

A lengthwise fold and single thickness is where the fabric is folded only part way across itself to cut both double and single layers. Measure the distance from foldline to edge in several places to be sure that it is equal, the fold is therefore on the straight grain.

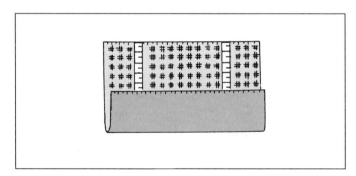

Two lengthwise folds is when the fabric is folded along its length so that the selvedges meet in the centre. This is used when a lot of the pattern pieces need to be placed on a fold.

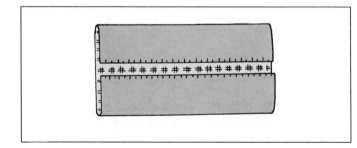

Fabrics that Require Special Handling

Napped or One-way Design Fabrics

Napped fabrics often reflect the light differently depending on which way up you hold them. It is therefore important to cut all the pieces the same way up. If the pile runs up the garment the colour is darker than if the pile runs down. The accepted way to make up this type of fabric, is with the pile running down. Cut out these fabrics following the 'with nap' layout diagrams on your instruction sheet.

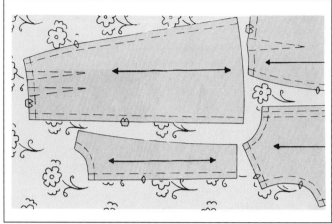

Other fabrics requiring the same treatment are plaids or stripes with a one-way repeat, printed or woven motifs with a one-way design, shot silks (where the warp and weft threads are in different colours) and some damasks and knits which can reflect the light differently depending on which way up they are held.

Designs that Must be Matched

Garments made from plaids, bold stripes, large and medium sized checks, border prints or large design motifs, must match at the seams. To accomplish this, you will have to make some adjustments to the cutting layout provided on your instruction sheet. In general, you will find it easier to work with the fabric folded right side out or on a single thickness with the right side facing up.

Extra yardage is required to accommodate this matching. How much extra depends on the size of the motif and the frequency of the repeat.

Positioning Bars or Motifs

Think about where you want the most prominent bar or motif to fall on your body. Beginning with the main front section, position the pattern pieces on the fabric so that:

1. Prominent vertical bars and large squares or motifs fall at the centre front and back of the garment, and at the centre of sleeves, yokes and collars.

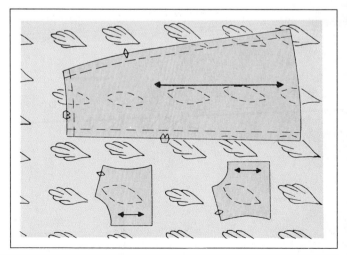

IV. Fabrics

2. Dominant horizontal bars fall at straight or slightly curved hemlines. As you do this observe what will happen on the rest of the garment - you may not want a repeat of the dominant bar or motif to fall at the fullest part of the bust, abdomen or hips.

3. In the case of a border print or large motif the hemline should fall just below the lower edge of the design.

4. Where possible motifs should not be chopped off at the seamlines.

5. The design matches vertically as well as horizontally (centre back of collar to centre back of garment).

As you lay out the first piece be sure that the grainline arrow is parallel to the selvedges or the bars of the design. Then position the remaining pattern pieces so that the adjoining pieces match at the seams.

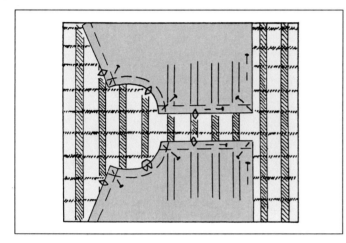

Some details cannot be matched no matter how hard you try. These include raglan sleeves, shoulder seams, darts, the back of the armhole seam, gathered or eased seams and circle skirts. Half circle skirts will chevron at the seams.

Plaids and Stripes

How you lay out a plaid or stripe depends on whether the design is regular or irregular. With a regular plaid or stripe the arrangement of bars is the same on both sides of the main bar, creating a regular design repeat.

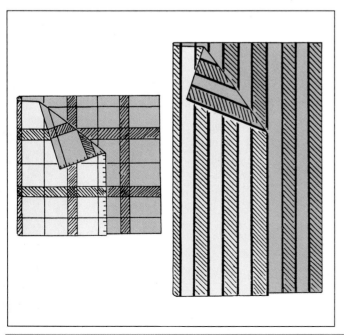

With an irregular plaid or stripe the arrangement or colour of bars is different on either side of the main bar creating an irregular repeat.

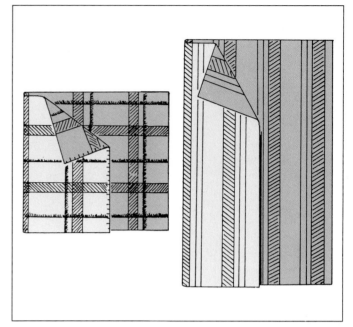

A regular pattern repeat can be cut out using the 'without nap' layout but an irregular repeat requires the 'with nap' layout.

When cutting through a double layer of fabric pin the stripes together at regular intervals to stop the fabric slipping and mismatching. Foldlines should be made along the centre of a main bar or group of bars.

Laying Out the Fabric

Roughly cut out all the tissue pattern pieces to within about 1.5 cm (1/2") of the cutting line, before positioning them on the fabric.

Some pattern brands do not have a cutting line, only a seamline. In which case first mark on the tissue the required seam allowance. This allows you the opportunity to take into consideration the type of fabric you are using and the type of seam you are sewing. But as a general rule, most patterns allow 1.5 cm (1/2") seam allowance all round.

1. Measure the distance from both ends of a grainline to the selvedge to check the pattern is placed as straight as possible.

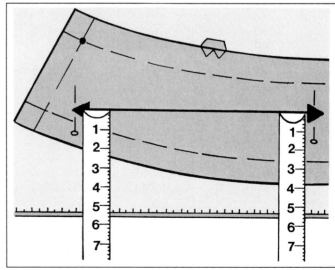

2. Check that all adjustments made to the pattern pieces (like lengthening or shortening) correspond with adjoining pieces, facings and linings.

3. Lay out **all** the pattern pieces before you start cutting to be sure that you have sufficient fabric.

4. Place pattern pieces printed side up, unless otherwise indicated on the diagram. Shading usually means that the piece is placed face down, (refer to pattern instruction sheet).

5. Pin pattern pieces in place with the pins at right angles to the pattern edge and diagonally at corners, for maximum stability. Space the pins 7 to 10 cm (3" to 4") apart.

6. Cut out using long sharp shears, (see Tools on page 6). Do **not** use pinking shears.

7. Cut around the notches (the diamond shapes) outwards. These marks are a vital aid to matching seams.

8. Mark all other markings with tailors tacks or chalk, (see Marking Methods on page 21).

9. Do not remove the pattern paper until you are ready to sew that piece.

Working with Special Fabrics

Leather

The Pattern

Keep to simple styles avoiding gathers and sharp pleats. For certain success make up and fit the pattern in cheap fabric first as leather cannot be successfully unpicked (the stitching leaves holes).

Cutting Out

Examine the skins for any weak areas or blemishes and mark these with chalk so that they can be avoided. Lay the pattern pieces on the reverse side of each single skin. Weight down the tissues (do not use pins because they make holes) and mark round the edges with felt tip pen. Leather does not have a grain so pieces can be layed any way to minimalise waste. But treat suede as a napped fabric and place the pattern pieces all one way. Cut out with sharp shears.

Marking

Pattern markings can be made with felt tip pen, soft pencil or tailors chalk.

Stitching

Soft leather (chamois, kid skin and fine suede) can be sewn with an ordinary sharp machine needle. Heavier leathers need a spear pointed 'leather' needle. Use a long stitch and instead of pinning or tacking/basting, hold the edges together with tape. If the leather does not pass smoothly under the machine foot, place a strip of tissue paper on top. For areas liable to stress, reinforce the seam with narrow cotton tape, to prevent stretching.

Pressing

Make sure the board is well padded. Seams can usually be finger pressed open; no neatening is needed - turnings can be stuck back in place with fabric adhesive. For pressing other areas, cover the leather with smooth brown paper and use a cool/warm iron. Do not use steam or a damp cloth.

Finishing

Hems can be pinked, scalloped, left plain or turned under once and either stitched by machine or stuck in position.

Lace

The Pattern

Use full, flowing styles for unlined lace. For tailored styles the lace can be backed with an opaque lining. Flimsy lace can be backed with matching net. Avoid too many seams, pockets and tight fitting sleeves.

Cutting Out

Plan the layout with care. On lace with a one-way motif treat it as a 'with nap' fabric and cut the pattern pieces in one direction. Lay the pattern pieces under the lace so that the motifs can be arranged to the best advantage.

When lace has a decorative edge, make use of it for a hemline or the top edge of a bodice.

For an opaque effect, cut out the pattern pieces again in lining fabric; tack/baste the lace and lining pieces together and make up as one.

Marking

Make tailors tacks in contrasting colours. If backing with lining, this can be chalk marked for speed.

Stitching

Use a fine needle for unlined lace. If the machine foot catches in open work lace, stitch through tissue paper.

Pressing

Pad ironing board with towelling to prevent flattening the lace pattern. Test for the best iron heat, steam or dry. Cover the fabric with a muslin press cloth.

Finishing

Unlined lace can be faced or bound at the edges with net to prevent possible show-through. Threaded loops can be substituted for buttonholes. Hemlines may be scalloped or finished with a narrow hem.

Fake Furs

The Pattern

Choose a bold clear-cut silhouette with raglan or set in sleeves and side seam pockets. Avoid bulky patch pockets, heavy collars, buttonholes and top-stitching and complicated styling details which will not show in fur.

Cutting Out

Pile fabrics must be cut with the pile in one direction - place all pattern pieces with the fur stroking downwards. Cut from a single layer, chalk round the pattern pieces on the reverse side of the cloth and cut out. Use the tips of the shears to snip through the backing fabric only (do not cut the fur).

Marking

Make tailors tacks in contrasting thread or chalk mark on the wrong side.

Stitching

Use a medium-sized machine needle and a medium to long stitch. Tack/baste seams firmly. Stitch in the direction of the pile. On the right side prise out any fur pile caught in the stitching using the point of a pin. Then on the wrong side trim the pile from seam allowances to reduce bulk. Cut deep darts open, and finish as for seams.

Pressing
Fake fur seams need little pressing, they open automatically. Press other sections face down on to layers of towelling to avoid crushing the pile.

Finishing
Use toggles, frogging or loops and buttons instead of button-holes. Replace any hidden facings with flat fabric for a smoother effect. If the backing fabric is stiff and hard to sew the hem can be stuck in position using fabric adhesive.

Sheers (Georgette, Chiffon, and Thin Silk)

The Pattern
Look for full, floaty shapes. Avoid too many seams, tailored or fitted lines, top-stitching and zips.

Cutting Out
Cover table with cloth to prevent slipping and pin the fabric to it at intervals. Use fine pins and place within the seam allowances only or use weights. Cut out with really sharp shears to prevent snagging.

Marking
Make tailors tacks in silk or finest tacking/basting cotton.

Stitching
Use the finest machine needle with a small stitch. Stitch through tissue paper to prevent the fabric puckering. Make either double-stitched or french seams, see pages 30 and 31.

Pressing
Make sure the iron and board are clean and smooth. Test press for the correct iron heat for the fibre; avoid steam, and use a thin muslin press cloth.

Finishing
Make tiny hand stitched buttonholes, with covered buttons or use rouleau loops in place of buttonholes. Hand stitch feather-weight zips in place. Hems should be very narrow, hand-rolled, or edge-stitched by machine.

Jersey

The Pattern
Your choice of pattern depends on the weight and stretchiness of the knitted fabric. Designs with fullness or drapes are best for fine jersey. For active sportswear the greater the stretch the better.

Cutting Out
Support excess length of fabric over a chair so that it does not pull out of shape. Use ball point pins in the seam allowances only. Cut out with sharp shears.

Marking
Use tailors tacks, chalk or dressmakers carbon.

Stitching
Use a ball-point machine needle and either a stretch stitch for seams which need to be flexible, or stretch the jersey on either side of the foot as you sew, using a straight stitch. Test stitch on off-cuts.

Pressing
For synthetic jersey use a cool dry iron, for extra moisture use a damp pressing cloth. Cotton jersey can be steamed with a warm iron. Take care not to stretch the jersey out of shape.

Finishing
Stabilise buttonhole areas with interfacing suitable for knitted fabrics before stitching them. To prevent seam allowances curling they can be double-stitched and trimmed down to half their width. On lightweight jerseys make a narrow hem, check it is level, then trim it to about 1 cm ($1/2$") and make two rows of stitching, one close to the folded hem edge, the second close to the raw edge. Alternatively, zig-zagging may be used to hold the narrow hem in place. Deeper hems are suitable on heavier jersey, turn once and blind-herringbone stitch in place, see page 28.

Some of the more sophisticated sewing machines will have additional stitches especially for sewing jersey fabrics, follow the manufacturer's instructions for these. Overlocking machines come into their own for sewing jersey fabrics.

Velvet or Corduroy

The Pattern
Look for simple styles with few seams, minimum detailing, and including a 'with nap' layout. Avoid top-stitching, pleats and too many buttonholes.

To cut down on bulk you can cut out any hidden facings in matching lining fabric - but remember to allow for this when buying your fabrics.

Cutting Out
Lay out pattern pieces so that the pile runs downwards on each piece. Cut thick velvets from a single layer, reversing the pattern after cutting one half. Use only fine steel pins and sharp shears.

Marking
Make tailors tacks with soft silky thread.

Stitching
Use a medium to fine machine needle. If you tack/baste seams take small stitches, and the occasional back-stitch. If the layers still tend to creep away when being stitched, separate the pile by placing tissue paper between the layers. Tear it away after stitching. Remove tacking/basting in short lengths.

Pressing
Test first on a spare piece (some velvets mark easily). Use a velvet needleboard, or place a spare piece of velvet face up on the ironing board; press with the garment pile-side-down. Steam-press **lightly** with iron at correct heat setting, do not handle velvet while damp.

Finishing
Use bound buttonholes or loops and buttons, see pages 75 to 82. Neaten seams and hems by over sewing or enclosing in binding.

Fabric weight and type	Needle size/Stitches per cm (inch)		Thread	
			General Sewing	**Top-stitching**
Very Light Chiffon, Lace, Organza, Georgette	70(9)/ 7-8 (16-20)	UK	Sylko, Sylko Supreme, Molnlycke Polyester	Sylko, Sylko Supreme, Molnlycke Polyester
		USA	Coats Cotton, Dual Duty Plus® Extra Fine	Coats Cotton, Dual Duty Plus® Extra Fine
		CAN	Coats Supersheen, Koban	Coats Supersheen, Koban
		AUS	Coats Supersheen	Coats Supersheen
Light to Medium Chambray, Challis, Crepe de chine, Fine jersey, Peau de soie, Gingham, Crepe	80(11)/ 5-7 (12-16)	UK	Sylko, Sylko Supreme, Molnlycke Polyester	Sylko, Sylko Supreme, Molnlycke Polyester
		USA	Coats Cotton, Dual Duty Plus® Extra Fine	Coats Cotton, Dual Duty Plus® All-purpose
		CAN	Coats Supersheen, Koban	Coats Supersheen, Koban
		AUS	Coats Supersheen	Coats Duet
Medium Linen, Poplin, Velvet, Corduroy, Broadcloth, Synthetic suede, some Double knits	80(11) or 90(14)/ 5-6 (12-14)	UK	Sylko, Sylko Supreme, Molnlycke Polyester	Sylko Bold
		USA	Coats Cotton, Dual Duty Plus® All-purpose	Coats Cotton, Dual Duty Plus® Topstitching and Buttonhole Twist
		CAN	Coats Supersheen, Koban	Coats Supersheen, Koban
		AUS	Coats Duet	Dual Duty
Medium Heavy Coating, Fake fur, Denim, Leather, Quilted fabrics, Sweater knits	90(14) or 100(16)/ 4-5 (10-12)	UK	Sylko, Sylko Supreme, Molnlycke Polyester	Sylko Bold
		USA	Coats Cotton, Dual Duty Plus® All-purpose	Coats Cotton, Dual Duty Plus® Topstitching and Buttonhole Twist
		CAN	Coats Supersheen, Koban	Coats Supersheen, Koban
		AUS	Coats Duet	Dual Duty
Heavy Canvas, Ticking, Sailcloth, Upholstery fabrics	110 (18)/ 3-4 (8-10)	UK	Sylko, Sylko Supreme, Molnlycke Polyester	Sylko Bold
		USA	Coats Cotton, Dual Duty Plus® Topstitching and Buttonhole Twist	Coats Cotton, Dual Duty Plus® Topstitching and Buttonhole Twist
		CAN	Coats Supersheen, Koban	Coats Supersheen, Koban
		AUS	Dual Duty	Dual Duty

Choosing the Right Thread

The thread you choose should be the same colour or a shade darker than your fabric. If you are using a plaid, print or tweed match the thread to the dominant colour in the fabric. The type of thread you should use will depend on the fabric (it is better to use a cotton thread on a natural fabric) and the stitching requirements. The table above is a guide to the thread, needle size and stitches per cm (inch) to be used for different types of fabric in the UK, the USA, Canada and Australia.

If a specific thread is not available **Tootal Craft** Sylko Supreme Multi-purpose thread in the **UK**, **Coats** Dual Duty Plus® All-purpose thread in the **USA**, **Coats** Koban thread in **Canada** and **Coats** Duet thread in Australia are recommended for all fabrics.

Marking Methods

A variety of marks and symbols are printed on the pattern tissue, all serving as guidelines for sewing details such as darts, pleats, zips and tucks. Do not be impatient, always transfer these, as they will save you time and frustration later.

Be sure to mark: dots, solid lines that indicate foldlines, pocket and buttonhole positions etc., (not the solid grainline arrows), centre front and back lines and broken lines indicating foldlines for pleats, tucks or fly openings etc.

Marking Pens

These are either water soluble or evaporating (the marks disappearing in under 48 hours. The disadvantage here is obvious!). They are used to pierce through all the layers of fabric, marking both sides simultaneously. If you choose to use one of these pens **test it first** on a scrap of fabric to be sure it will not leave a permanent discolouration.

Dressmaker Pencils

The brush on the end is for removing the chalk-like crayon from the fabric after use. It is, however, advisable to make marks on the wrong side of the fabric where possible, marking each layer separately. Starting at the outside edge and working in, stick a pin vertically through the pattern paper and fabric layers to mark a spot accurately. Separate the layers (without removing the pin) and mark with the crayon.

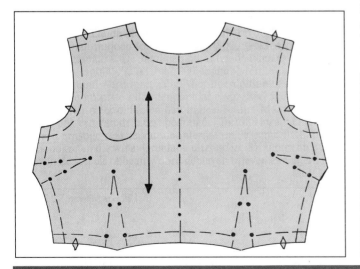

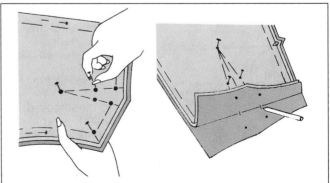

V. Preliminaries

Tracing Paper and Tracing Wheels

Read the manufacturer's instructions carefully to see if the markings are removable. Some can only be used on the wrong side of the fabric. The paper is inserted like carbon paper between the layers to be marked, and the teeth of the wheel used to punch the marks.

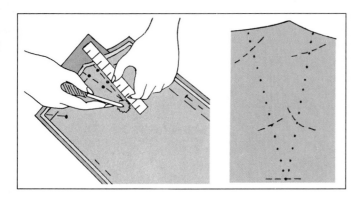

Tailors Tacks

This is by far the safest method and suitable for all types of fabric especially delicates, velvet or knobbly tweed. Choose a tacking/basting thread in a contrasting colour to your fabric. Using a long double strand of thread without a knot, make a small running stitch in the fabric at the dot mark, then sew another stitch crossing over the first but leaving a large loop. As you move on to the next dot mark leave a loose thread. Repeat at each mark. Cut the loops and the long threads connecting each mark. Separate the fabric layers carefully and snip the threads between the layers leaving tufts on either side.

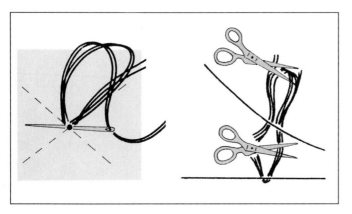

Snip Marking

This is a fast way to mark the ends of darts, foldlines, pleats and tucks, centre front and centre back. It is also an alternative way to mark notches. Just make a small snip in the seam allowance (no more than 3 mm (^{1}/8") deep) at the marking point.

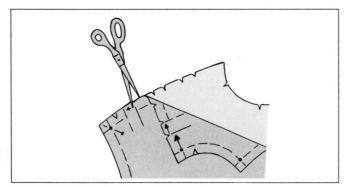

Mastering Your Sewing Machine

Whether your machine is a basic straight stitch model or one of the computerised 'state of the art' variety, it is the most valuable piece of sewing equipment to have. With any machine it is possible to produce professional looking garments at a fraction of the cost of shop bought items. All you need is a little know-how and practice.

Because the features and capabilities of machines vary among models and manufacturers, your best guide is the instruction manual which comes with the machine.

Good quality stitching is dependent on having the correct tension, pressure, needle size and stitch length. Many machines now have a universal setting which is correct for most sewing jobs. But you may need to adjust it for some fabrics or sewing tasks. To ensure the best results always test stitch on off-cuts of the fabric you are using for your garment.

Thread Tension

Tension refers to the amount of drag or tautness exerted on both the needle thread and the bobbin thread as they move through the sewing machine. When the tension is correctly set, the stitches should be perfectly balanced, the two threads interlocking in the centre of the fabric so that the stitches look the same on both sides of the fabric.

If the tension is not balanced, your manual will tell you how to correct it by adjusting the needle tension. Most tension problems can be solved by adjusting the needle tension to match the bobbin tension. Although some machines have a screw on the bobbin case that controls the bobbin tension, most manufacturers do not recommend adjusting this.

To test for balanced tension, thread the machine with different colour threads in the needle and the bobbin. Take a scrap of fabric and fold it along the bias. Stitch a line about 1.5 cm (^{1}/2") in from the fold then pull the fabric until the thread breaks.

If both the bobbin and the needle thread break then the tension is correct.

If only the bobbin thread breaks that means that the bobbin tension is tighter than the needle tension.

To remedy, tighten the needle tension to match that of the bobbin.

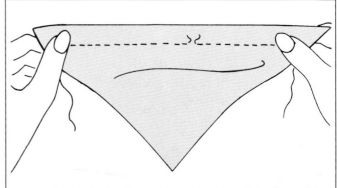

If only the needle thread breaks, that means that the needle tension is tighter than the bobbin tension.

To remedy, loosen the needle tension to match that of the bobbin.

Presser Foot

The presser foot exerts pressure on the fabric as it moves between the presser foot and the feed bed. The amount of pressure needed can be affected by the fabric's weight, bulk, texture or finish. If the pressure is correctly set for the fabric, both layers will move through the machine at the same rate. If the fabric persistently puckers in front of the foot the pressure is probably too tight. If the fabric slips about even when the foot is down you may need to increase the pressure.

Stitch Length

The stitch length is easily changed on every machine. It is advisable to experiment for the most suitable stitch size on a scrap of fabric before sewing your garment.

The weight of the fabric is important in determining the stitch length to be used. Generally the lighter the fabric the shorter the stitch length and the heavier the fabric the longer the stitch length. However if the fabric has texture further adjustments may be required.

Stitching Techniques

Before attempting to make a garment familiarise yourself with your sewing machine. Follow the manufacturer's handbook instructions and practise simple seams. Start as follows:

1. Grasp the needle and bobbin threads with one hand and gently pull them under, then behind or to the side of the presser foot.

2. Place the fabric under the presser foot so that the right edge is aligned with the desired marking on the plate. The bulk of the fabric should be to the left of the presser foot.

3. Turn the wheel to lower the needle into the fabric near the beginning of the seamline.

4. While still holding the thread tails, lower the presser foot and begin stitching with a slow, even speed. Continue to hold on to the thread tails until you have stitched for about 2.5 cm (1").

5. Release the thread tails and continue stitching.

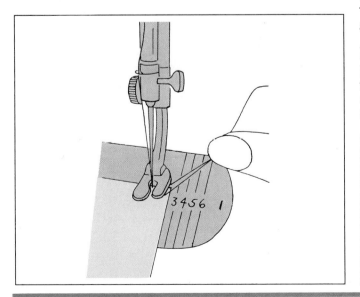

Guiding the Fabric

Rest one hand on the fabric in front of the presser foot, and the other hand behind the presser foot. Use both hands to gently guide the fabric through the machine as you stitch. Do not push or pull the fabric. At the same time keep your eye on the cut edge of the fabric, rather than on the needle. This helps you to keep the stitching straight.

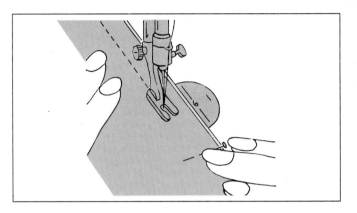

Accuracy

The easiest way to maintain accurate stitching is to align the right edge of the fabric with a guide line. You can use one of the lines etched in the plate on your machine or make your own mark with a piece of tape stuck on the plate at a measured distance from the needle hole. The edge of the foot is useful as a guide for stitching very close to an edge.

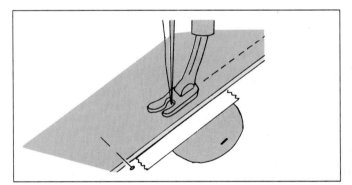

Securing the Stitching

To prevent the stitching from coming undone at the beginning and end of the seam, use one of the following techniques:

Back-stitch

Insert the needle a little bit in from the start of the seam, set the machine to stitch in reverse and back-stitch. Set the machine to stitch forward and complete the seam. Slow down near the end of the seam and back-stitch again.

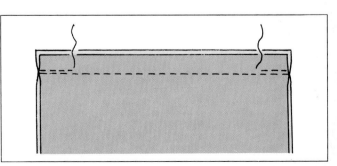

VI. Stitches and Seams

Tie the threads

This technique is useful for the point of darts or if your machine does not stitch in reverse. Leave at least 10 cm (4") long thread tails at the beginning and end of the stitching.

Before tying the threads, it may be necessary to bring both tails of thread to the same side of the fabric. To do this, tug gently on one thread until the loop of the other thread appears, then insert a pin through the loop and draw it up. Tie the ends in a knot.

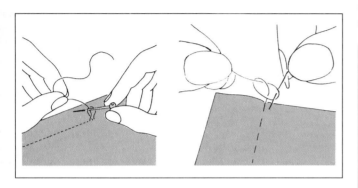

Stitching Terms

Gathering

This can be done by hand or machine. Set your machine to its longest stitch setting (you may find it also helps to loosen the needle tension slightly) and stitch two rows 5 mm (1/4") apart, both inside of the seam allowance. Draw up the fabric by pulling the bobbin threads, (see Gathering on page 38).

Ease-stitching

This technique is used when you are joining a longer garment edge to a slightly shorter one. It is similar to gathering but there should be no folds or gathers visible on the right side when the seam is stitched. Stitch a single row with the machine on its longest stitch length close to the seamline inside the seam allowance.

1. Stitch slightly beyond the notches which indicate the area to be eased.

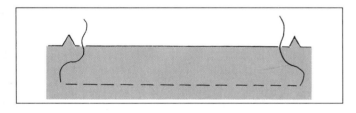

2. Pin this section to the adjoining section, matching notches, and draw up the fabric to fit by pulling the bobbin thread, distributing fullness evenly.

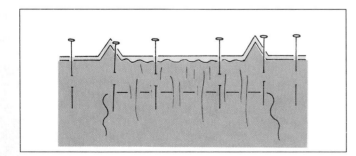

3. Re-set your machine and stitch the seam with the eased section on top.

Edge-stitching

This row of stitches appears on the outside of the garment and is often used to keep edges of collars crisp. It is placed approximately 2 mm (1/8") or less away from a seamline or foldline, or close to a finished edge. Although it is similar to top-stitching, edge-stitching is less noticable because it is closer to the edge and it is usually done in matching thread.

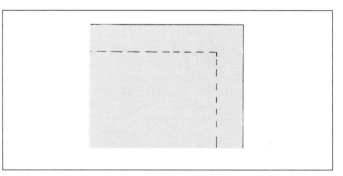

Reinforcement stitching

This technique strengthens the stitching in areas that will be closely trimmed, such as corners, or along deep curves that will be clipped or notched at frequent intervals. The principle is simple - just sew with a shorter stitch length.

At an outward corner, reduce the stitch length for about 2.5 cm (1") on either side of the corner.

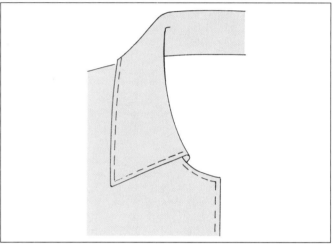

At an inward corner, reduce the stitch length for 2.5 cm (1") on either side of the corner, then clip just to the stitching, (see joining an inward corner to an outward corner on page 33).

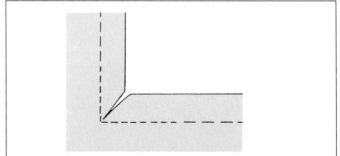

Stay-stitching

This row of stitches prevents curved or bias edges, such as necklines, shoulders, and waistlines, from stretching out of shape as they are handled prior to final stitching. Where required stay-stitching should be the very first operation before joining any seams.

To stay-stitch, stitch close to the seamline inside the seam allowance. On deep curves shorten the stitch length so that the stay-stitching doubles as reinforcement stitching.

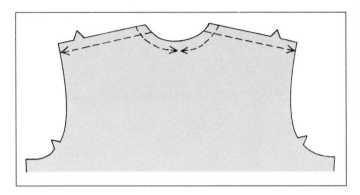

To prevent the edge of the fabric from stretching as you stay-stitch, stitch in the same direction as the fabric weave. As a guideline, you may find arrows printed on the instruction sheet illustrations or along the seamline on the pattern tissue. If there are no arrows to direct you, you can determine which way to stitch by running your finger along the cut edge. The yarns will lie smoothly in one direction. Stitch in that direction.

Pinning and Tacking/Basting

There are several ways of holding the fabric layers in place prior to stitching and each depends upon the type of fabric or seam.

Pinning

This is the quickest and easiest method and fine for most seams.

Place pins at right angles to the seamline, 2.5 to 7.5 cm (1" to 3") apart. Insert the pins so that you take small bites of fabric right at the seamline. The heads should be to the right of the presser foot so that they can be efficiently removed as you stitch, (unless you are left-handed).

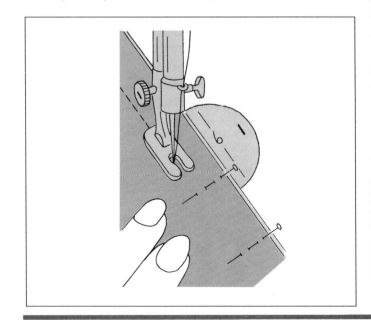

Fabric Fusing

Fabric fusing is a fast way to hold fabric layers in place for hand finishing or top-stitching.

Cut a strip of fusible web the desired length. Sandwich it between the two fabric layers and fuse, holding the iron in place for only a few seconds.

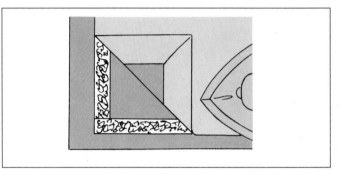

Follow the manufacturer's recommendations for heat and steam. Fusible web can also be used as a quick and easy hemming method, (see page 49).

Machine Tacking/Basting

This is most often used to sew a garment together temporarily in order to check the fit.

1. Pin the fabric layers together, matching the markings.

2. Loosen the needle thread tension, adjust the stitch setting to the longest length, and stitch. Do not bother to secure the stitching at the ends of the seams.

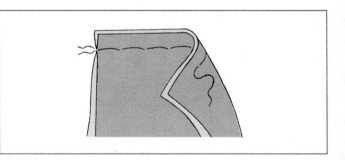

To remove the tacking/basting easily, clip the needle thread every 2.5 cm (1") or so, then pull out the bobbin thread. If you are doing a lot of machine tacking/basting, you could use different coloured threads in the bobbin and the needle to make it easier to know which thread to clip and which to pull.

Hand Tacking/Basting

Hand tacking/basting is a secure method of holding fabric layers temporarily in place. It is frequently used in detail areas where pinning would not be accurate or secure enough and machine tacking/basting would be difficult to do. It can also be used on sheer or very slippery fabrics.

For the firmest holding power weave the needle in and out of the fabric so that the stitches and the spaces between them are all the same size - approximately 5 mm (1/4") long.

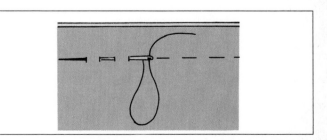

VI. Stitches and Seams

For areas that do not need to be so secure, make the stitches 5 mm (¼") long and the spaces between 1.5 cm (½") long.

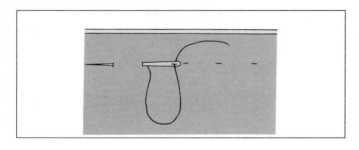

Double-sided or Basting Tape

This is a valuable aid when you need to match up plaids or stripes, or for the positioning of pockets or zips. To match a design at the seamline:

1. Press one seam allowance under at the seamline.

2. Position the tape so that the sticky side is against the right side of the seam allowance about 2 to 3 mm (⅛") from the fold.

3. Remove the protective covering from the tape. Lap the pressed seam allowance over the unpressed one, matching both the seamline and the fabric design.

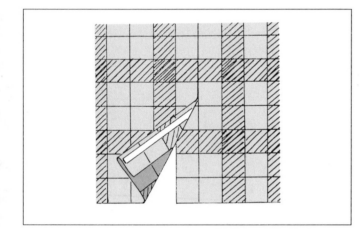

4. Open out the folded seam allowance and stitch the seam in the usual way following the crease line.

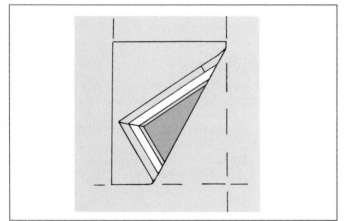

Stitching in the Seam Groove

This technique is a quick way to hold layers of fabric in place at the seams. It is an effective way to secure neckline, armhole or waistband facings, as well as fold-up cuffs.

Press seam allowances open, then on the outside of the garment stitch in the groove formed by the seam, trying not to catch the fabric surface. Be sure to catch all the underneath layers in their correct position in your stitching.

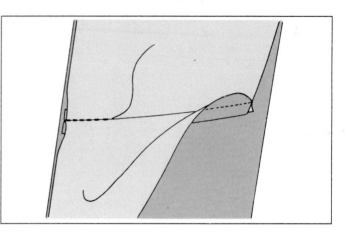

Top-stitching

This is an extra row of stitching on the outside of the garment along or near a finished edge. Although top-stitching is usually added as decoration, it can also be functional. For example, it can be used to attach a patch pocket or to help keep seam allowances flat on hard-to-press fabrics.

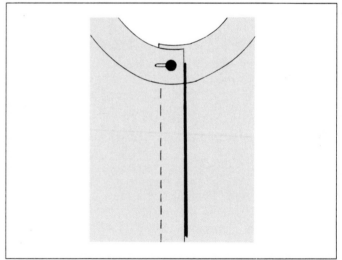

1. Use a matching or contrasting thread as desired. A thicker buttonhole thread could be used.

2. Stitch with a slightly longer stitch.

3. To keep your stitching straight, use one of the methods described under Accuracy on page 23.

4. Before top-stitching, test stitch using the same number of layers of fabric (including linings or interfacings).

To make each stitch more pronounced, you may want to slightly loosen the needle thread tension. You may also need to adjust the presser foot pressure to accommodate the extra bulk.

Under-stitching

This row of stitching prevents an inside layer of fabric, usually a facing, from rolling to the outside of the garment.

Under-stitching is done after the seam allowances are trimmed, graded, clipped or notched.

1. Press the seam allowances towards the facing.

2. On the right side of the garment, stitch 2 mm ($1/8$") from the seamline, through the facing and seam allowances only.

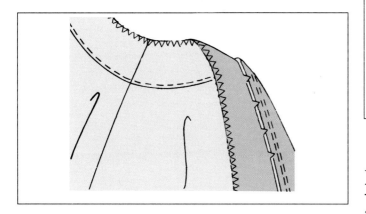

Hand Stitches

Running Stitch

This is used for gathering, tucking, mending and for seams that are not under strain.

Weave the needle in of the fabric several times before pulling the needle through the fabric. The stitches and spaces should be the same length, about 2 to 3 mm ($1/8$") in length for seams and 3 to 6 mm ($1/4$") for gathering.

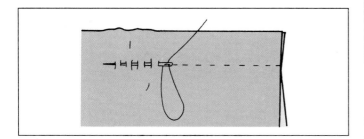

Backstitch

This stitch is used to secure beginnings and ends of hand sewn seams, as well as for repairing seams. There are many variations, but all are worked by inserting the needle into the fabric behind the thread.

1. With right sides of the fabric together fasten the thread on the underside of the fabric and bring the needle up through all the layers.

2. Insert the needle back down through the fabric, 2 mm ($1/8$") behind the point where it first emerged.

3. Bring the needle up again 2 mm ($1/8$") ahead of the first stitch. Continue along the length of the seam.

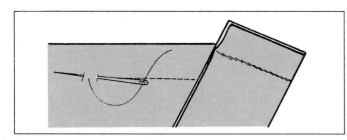

Half Backstitch

Worked in the same way as backstitch except the that the stitches and the distance between them is not equal.

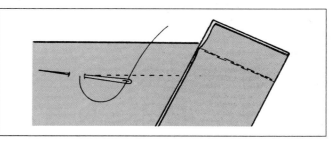

Prick Stitch

This is a form of backstitch, and is useful if you wish to insert a zip by hand into a delicate or hard to handle fabric. Use it in place of the final top-stitching.

1. Fasten the thread on the underside of the fabric and bring the needle up through all the layers.

2. Insert the needle back down through the fabric, a thread or two behind the point where it first emerged.

3. Bring the needle up again about 5 mm ($1/4$") ahead of the first stitch. Continue along the length of the seam.

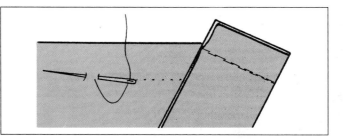

Over Sewing

This stitch (also known as overcasting) is used to finish raw edges and is worked by inserting the needle at an angle, from the back to the front of a single layer of fabric.

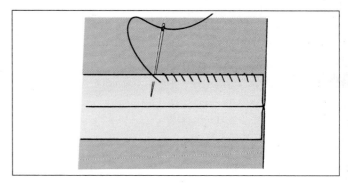

Slip-stitch

This is used for securing cuffs and waistbands, and all turned under edges, because the stitches are invisible on both the inside and outside of the garment.

1. Fasten the thread to the folded edge of the fabric.

VI. Stitches and Seams

2. Working from right to left, pick up a single fabric thread just below the folded edge.

3. Insert the needle into the fold directly above the first stitch and bring it out 5 mm (¹/₄") away.

4. Pick up another thread in the garment directly below the point where the needle emerged and continue in this way, alternating between garment and fold.

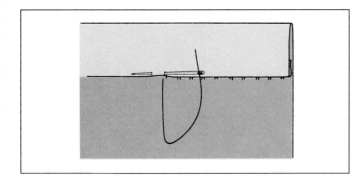

Whip Stitch

This is used to hold two edges together or to hold a facing in place by attaching it to a seam allowance.

The needle is inserted from back to front, at right angles to the finished edges. The distance between the stitches can vary depending on the task.

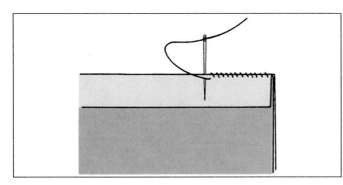

Hand Hemming Stitches

Hemming Stitch

This stitch is used for all types of hemming, particularly on hems finished with seam binding or for unlined garments.

1. Secure the sewing thread at a seam.

2. Take a tiny inconspicuous stitch in the garment, then bring the needle diagonally up through the edge of the seam binding or hem edge.

3. Continue spacing the stitches about 5 mm (¹/₄") apart.

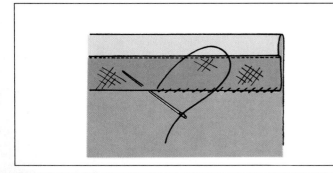

Blind-herringbone Stitch

This stitch is good for hemming heavy fabrics or jerseys as it has built in stretch.

1. Finish the raw edge of the hem (see page 33) and roll it back by about 5 mm (¹/₄"). Fasten the thread to the rolled edge.

2. Working from left to right, make a small horizontal stitch in the underside of the hem close to the edge, through a single thickness of material.

3. Then make another stitch into the main part of the garment diagonally across from the first stitch.

4. Continue to zig-zag along the hem edge keeping the threads loose.

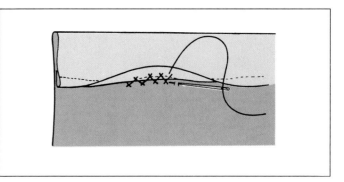

Blind-hemming Stitch

This is used for invisible hemming and holding facings in place.

1. Finish the raw edge of the hem (see page 33) and roll it back by about 5 mm (¹/₄"). Fasten the thread to the rolled edge.

2. Make a small horizontal stitch under one thread of the garment then another from the underside of the hem (or facing) diagonally above.

3. Continue in this manner being careful not to pull the stitches tight.

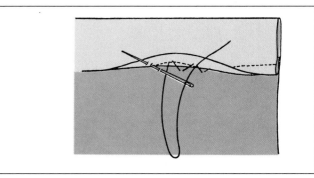

Decorative Stitches

The addition of embroidery stitches to a garment can be a very effective form of surface decoration. It is especially popular on children's clothes, but can also give an individual finish to many other types of garment.

Mark the design on to the right side of the fabric with a tacking/basting thread or tailors chalk and work the design using embroidery thread and a selection of the following stitches. Secure the thread to the underside of the fabric.

Blanket Stitch

This stitch can be worked over an edge as a method of finishing a raw edge. When used as a decorative stitch mark two parallel lines. Working from left to right, bring the needle out on the lower line, insert the needle on the top line, a little to the right. Bring it out on the lower line directly below, keeping the thread under the point of the needle pull the needle through.

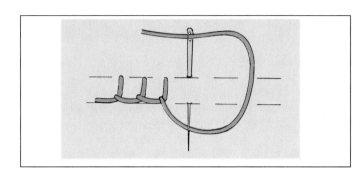

Chain Stitch

Bring the needle to the right side and working from right to left, looping the thread insert the needle where the thread emerges and bring it out a short distance away, keeping the working thread under the point of the needle.

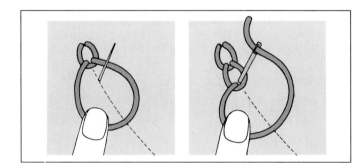

Lazy Daisy Stitch

The stitches are formed in the same way as chain stitch, but working from the centre and fastening each loop with a small stitch.

Cross Stitch

Bring the needle out at A, insert it at B, then out at C, and into

D, repeat as required. To work the other diagonal bring the needle out at E, insert it at B and so on.

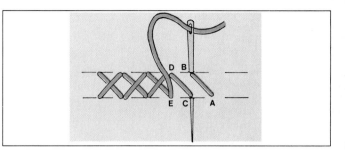

Feather Stitch

Bring the needle to the right side of the fabric and to the right of the marked line. Holding the thread, take a small diagonal stitch above the thread on the left of the line, repeat on the opposite side of the line. Continue, working on alternate sides of the line.

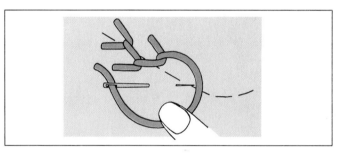

French Knot

Bring the needle to the right side, holding the thread down with the left hand, wrap the yarn around the needle twice, take the needle to the wrong side close to where it emerged and pull the thread through leaving a small knot.

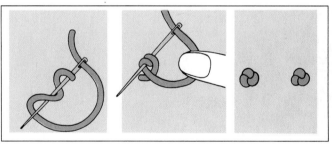

Herringbone Stitch

Working from left to right, bring the needle to the right side at A, insert the needle at B and make a small stitch to the left (C), insert the needle at D and make a small stitch to the left (E).

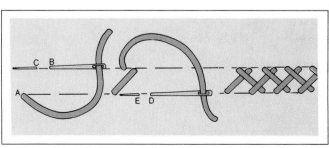

VI. Stitches and Seams

Satin Stitch

Work parallel straight stitches close together over the shape. A slightly raised effect can be achieved by first working running stitches over the area.

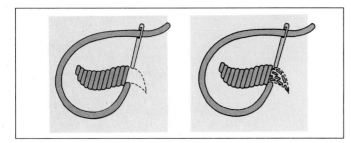

Stem Stitch

Working from left to right along the design line, bring the needle to the right side of the line, take a small stitch and return the needle to the left of the previous stitch.

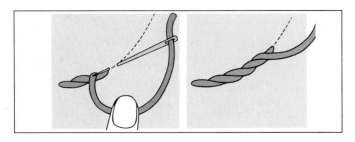

Decorative Reinforcement Stitches

These decorative stitches are used for tailored garments to reinforce the ends of pockets and pleats. First mark a triangular shape on the right side, and secure the thread within it.

Arrowheads

Bring the needle out at A, take a small stitch from right to left at B, then into C and out at A, just to the right of the previous thread. Continue in this way until the triangle is filled.

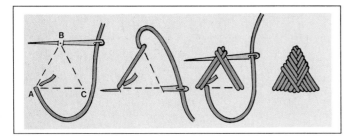

Crows Foot

Bring the needle out at A, take a small stitch from right to left at B, then a small stitch from left to right at C, across to A and a small stitch from left to right. Continue in this way until the triangle is filled.

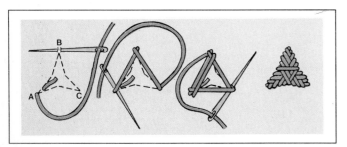

Types of Seams

Although the plain seam is the one you will use most often, there are other choices. You may want a specific decorative look or be using a fabric that requires special handling. The plain seam usually requires a seam finish. However many of the other seams incorporate the seam finish into the seam technique.

Note: Your pattern instructions will probably utilise a plain seam but you have the option of changing that. Always make a sample seam in some scraps of your fabric before you begin.

Plain Seam

With right sides together, stitch along the seamline, which is usually 1.5 cm (1/2") from the cut edge.

For jersey, stretch the fabric slightly as you sew.

Press the seam allowances open and finish as appropriate, (see Seam Finishes on page 33).

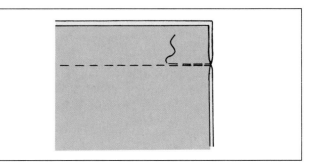

Double-stitched Seam

This is a combination seam and edge finish that creates a narrow seam especially suitable for sheers and knits. To prevent the fabric from fraying, it is stitched twice.

1. Stitch a plain seam.
2. Stitch again 3 mm (1/8") away, within the seam allowance, using a straight or zig-zag stitch.
3. Trim close to the second row of stitching.
4. Press the seam allowances to one side.

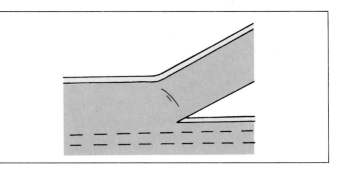

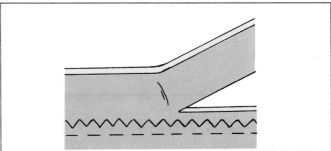

Stretch Fabric Seams

Stretch fabrics need seams that are supple enough to 'give' with the fabric. You can sew them with straight stitches, zig-zag stitches or one of the stretch stitches built in to many machines.

Listed below are some variations, utilising the straight stitch and the zig-zag:

1. Stitch a plain seam, stretching the fabric slightly as you sew.

2. For extra strength, stitch a double-stitched seam.

3. For greater stretch use a narrow, medium length zig-zag stitch to sew along the seamline. Then zig-zag 5 mm (1/4") away within the seam allowance, and trim close to the last line of stitching.

If your machine has a built in stretch stitch, consult your manual for instructions. For over edge stretch stitches the seam allowances must be trimmed before stitching.

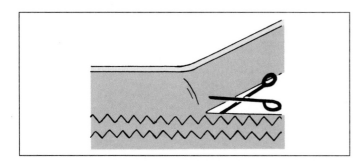

Stabilising stretch fabric

Seams at the neckline, shoulders and waistlines, should **not** stretch because the garment will lose its shape. Stabilise them by stitching seam binding or twill tape into the seams.

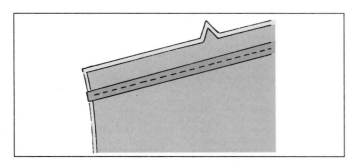

Flat-felled Seam

The flat-felled seam is frequently used on sportswear, menswear and reversible garments.

1. With **wrong** sides of the fabric together, stitch a plain seam and press the seam allowances to one side. Trim the underneath seam allowance to 2 mm (1/8").

2. Turn under 5 mm (1/4") of the top seam allowance and pin or tack/baste in place on right side of the garment over the trimmed edge.

3. Edge-stitch close to the fold, through the seam allowance and the garment.

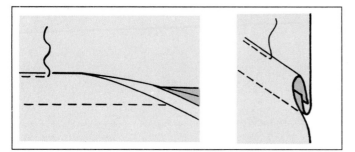

French Seam

This seam adds a couture look to the inside of garments made from sheers and lightweight silks. The finished seam, which should be very narrow, completely encloses the raw edges of the seam allowances.

1. With **wrong** sides together make a seam 1 cm (1/2") from the edge.

2. Trim the seam allowances to a scant 3 mm (1/8"), then press them open.

3. Fold the fabric right sides together along the stitching line; press.

4. Stitch 5 mm (1/4") from the fold. Press the seam open, with the allowances to one side.

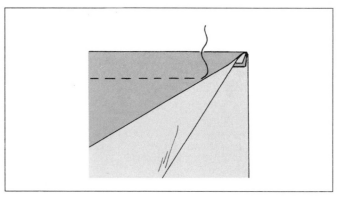

Lapped Seam

This type of seam is frequently used on non-woven fabrics, such as synthetic or real suede and leather, because their edges do not fray.

1. Trim away the seam allowance on the upper (overlap) section, before stitching the seam.

2. Lap the edge over the underneath section, placing the trimmed edge along the seamline; hold it in place with double-sided tape or fusible web.

3. Edge-stitch along the trimmed edge. Top-stitch on the overlap, 5 mm (1/4") away from the first stitching.

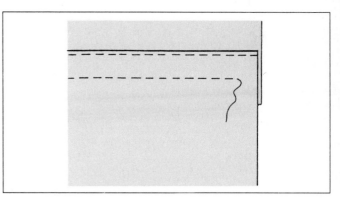

Top-stitched Seam

This treatment accents the seamlines. It also helps to keep the seam allowances flat - a great benefit when you are working with crease-resistant fabrics.

1. Stitch a plain seam and press open.

VI. Stitches and Seams

2. Working on the right side of the garment, top-stitch on both sides of the seam, 2 to 5 mm (¹/8" to ¹/4") from the seamline.

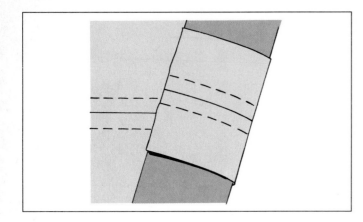

As an alternative, stitch a plain seam, press the seam allowances to one side and top-stitch 2 to 5 mm (¹/8" to ¹/4") away from the seam, through all layers.

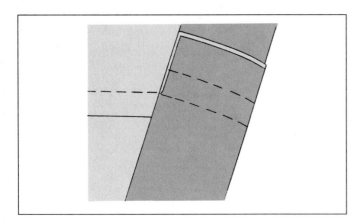

Welt Seam

This type of seam is good for reducing bulk and holding seam allowances flat on heavyweight fabrics. From the outside it looks like a top-stitched seam.

1. Stitch a plain seam and press the seam allowances to one side.

2. Trim the underneath seam allowance to a scant 5 mm (¹/4").

3. On the right side, top-stitch 5 mm (¹/4") from the seam, enclosing the untrimmed seam allowance.

4. For a double-welt seam, also edge-stitch close to the seamline, this looks like a flat-felled seam.

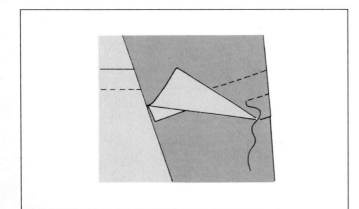

Seam Techniques

Intersecting Seams

When one seam or dart will be crossed by another (for example, side seams crossed by a waist seam or the inside corners of a waistband) diagonally trim the ends of the first seam allowance or dart to reduce the bulk.

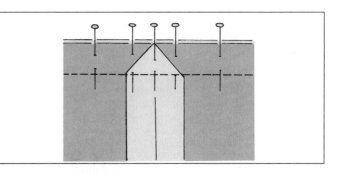

Bias Seams

To join two bias edges (such as the side seam of a bias cut skirt) hold the fabric in front of and behind the presser foot and stretch it very slightly as you stitch. Although this allows the seam to 'give' as you stitch, it will also relax into a smooth seam when you are finished.

Corners

To strengthen seams at corners, shorten the stitch length for about 2.5 cm (1") on either side of the corner. This reinforcement stitching helps to prevent the corner from fraying after it is trimmed and turned right side out.

To stitch perfect corners it helps to mark with chalk where the two seamlines intersect. Then stitch to this point and with the needle still in the fabric, raise the presser foot, pivot the fabric to the correct position to finish the seam, lower the presser foot and continue stitching.

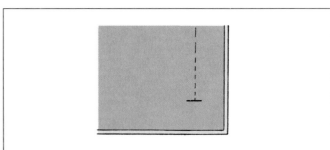

For sharp outward corners

For example on a collar point, take one or two diagonal stitches across the point instead of stitching right up to it. Trim across the point first, then trim diagonally on either side.

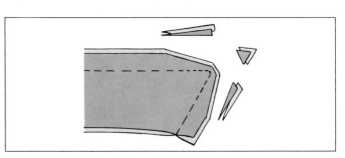

For inward corners

Reinforce the inward corner with small stitches and clip just to the stitching.

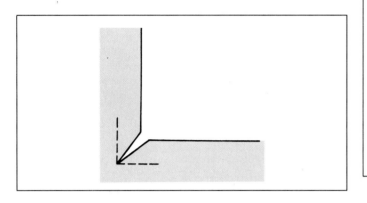

To join an inward corner to an outward corner

1. For example on a yoke reinforce and clip the inward corner as given above.

2. Pin the two sections together matching seamlines and markings, with the clipped section on top.

3. Stitch to the corner. Leave the needle in the fabric, raise the presser foot and pivot the fabric so that the clipped edge spreads apart and the cut edges of the fabric match.

4. Lower the presser foot and continue stitching.

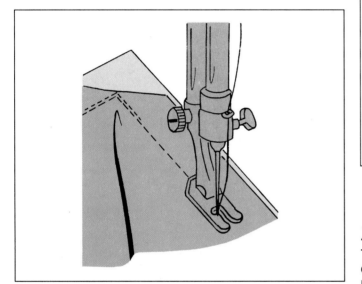

Seam Finishes

To prevent fraying and add durability, plain seams usually require some type of seam finish. If the garment is going to be lined, or if the fabric is very tightly woven, no seam finish is required. The following seam finishes can also be used to edge facings and hems. Also see Over Sewing on page 27.

Stitch and Pink

This is the quickest method for finishing fabrics that do not fray easily.

1. Stitch 5 mm (¹/₄") from each seam allowance edge.

2. Trim close to the stitching with pinking shears.

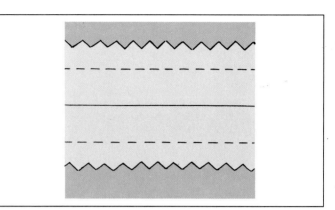

Turned and Stitched

This method of finishing is not suitable for bulky fabrics.

1. Turn under the raw edges of the seam allowance by 3 to 5 mm (¹/₈" to ¹/₄") depending on how much the fabric frays and press.

2. Stitch close to the fold.

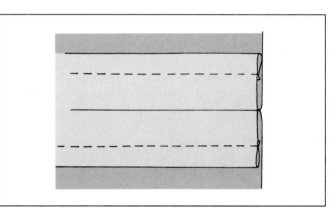

Zig-zag

This is a good choice for most fabrics, including heavyweight ones that fray. Experiment with the stitch length and width, using a smaller width for lightweight fabrics, and a larger one for heavyweights.

Zig-zag over, or as close as possible to each raw edge. If your machine has an overcast stitch, you can use it in place of the zig-zag stitch.

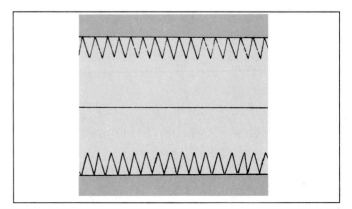

VI. Stitches and Seams

Straight Stitch

Use this finish on knits that curl, jersey and stretch towelling. Do not use pinking shears on knit fabrics, it is unnecessary work and may cause the fabric to curl. To minimise curling, finish the seams **before** stitching them.

Stitch 5 mm (1/4") from the raw edges.

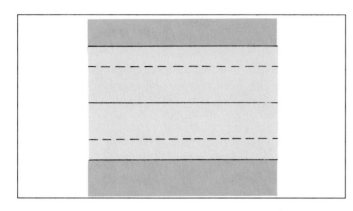

Bound Edges

This is a custom finish that is suitable for any fabric. However, if the fabric frays a great deal, bind the seam allowances before stitching the seams. (Chalk mark your notches). Use a lightweight double fold bias binding. Also see Attatching Your Own Binding or Double Fold Bias Tape on page 44.

1. Position the tape over seam allowance and secure with pins.

2. Stitch close to the edge, removing pins as you go and ensuring you sew through both edges of tape at once. You can use a straight stitch, but for best results, particularly on fabrics that fray use a narrow zig-zag stitch.

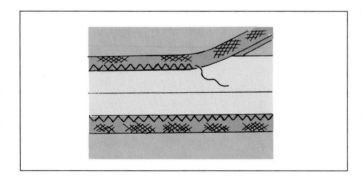

Trimming and Clipping

Not all good sewing techniques are centred around the sewing machine. Your scissors are an invaluable aid to professional results. Thanks to them, your garment can have crisper corners, flatter edges, and smoother curves and seams.

It is vitally important to trim and/or clip certain seam turnings:

1. In areas such as the underarm section of an armhole seam where the wider seam allowance would interfere with the fit.

2. When a special seam technique, such as a french seam or a welt seam requires it, (see pages 31 and 32).

3. On enclosed seams as a preliminary step to grading.

4. To eliminate excess fabric at the seam allowances of corners and points. That way, they will be smooth and flat once they are turned right side out.

Grading or Layering

This refers to the process of trimming each seam allowance to a different width so that the layers will not create ridges on the outside of the garment. This technique is most commonly used on enclosed seams, such as those sometimes found along collar, cuff, pocket and faced edges. If the fabric is lightweight, grading is usually not necessary, trimming is enough. However, if the fabric is medium to heavyweight, all enclosed seams must be trimmed and graded. Corners require special treatment, (see pages 32 and 33).

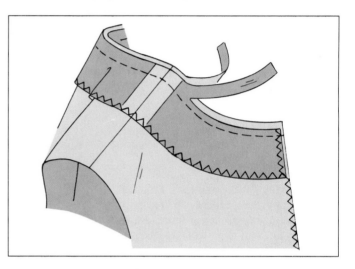

Clipping and Notching

This is how you use scissors to make curved seams lie flat.

On inward, or concave curves, make little clips or snips in the seam allowance just to, but not through, the stitching.

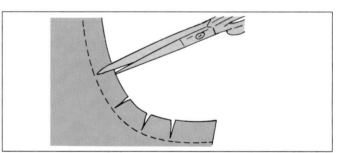

On outward, or convex curves, cut wedge-shaped notches from the seam allowance to eliminate excess fullness when a seam is pressed open.

On a flat curved seam, when you are joining an inward curve to an outward curve, you would clip one seam allowance to release the fabric and notch the other to eliminate the fullness.

Basic Constructions

These are the basic techniques required to construct most garments. They will be an invaluable aid to all your dressmaking tasks.

Pressing

Careful pressing is as important as accurate stitching if you want professional results. You are pressing when you lift the iron up and then replace it on to the fabric in an overlapping pattern. This differs from ironing, where the iron is pushed back and forth over the fabric. Ironing can distort the fabric, pressing will not.

To achieve the best results **press as you go**. Do not cross two seams without having first pressed the original seam open. Ideally your ironing board should be set up close to your sewing machine. Organise your sewing so that you work on several sections at one time, and then press everything that needs it at the same time.

1. Always test the pressing method on a scrap of fabric before pressing the actual garment.

2. Make sure the fabric is straight and as smooth as possible before starting.

3. Remove pins before pressing, they could leave impressions on the fabric or damage the iron. Tacking/basting stitches can also leave impressions and so they should also be removed before pressing.

4. As a rule it is best to use light pressure, without resting the full weight of the iron on the fabric. Do **not** over press, you may damage the fabric and cause it to shine.

Pressing Seams

1. Press flat along stitching line before opening the seam to blend the stitches.

2. Press the seam allowances open or to one side, as indicated in the pattern instructions. Try using only the tip of the iron, rather than the full plate, to prevent the edges of the seam allowances showing through on the right side.

3. Press the seam or detail area from the right side, protecting the fabric with a press cloth if necessary.

Finger Pressing

Some delicate fabrics or fabrics with a texture that could be flattened, such as velvet or fake furs can be finger pressed. To do this, hold the iron above the fabric and apply a generous amount of steam. Then use your fingers, not the iron, to press seams, darts and edges, (see table below).

Pressing Equipment

In addition to your iron and ironing board there is also a wide range of equipment to help with this process.

Press cloths These are used to prevent shine and water spots on the garment fabric, or dampened to give extra moisture when pressing. Ideally press cloths should be the same weight of fabric as your garment, in muslin or cotton, a linen tea cloth would be a suitable substitute.

Teflon iron cover This is useful for pressing certain fabrics at high temperatures without burning, shining or marking with a damp pressing cloth.

Pressing Guide				
Fibre	**Pressure**	**Heat**	**Moisture**	**Special Instructions**
Acetate	Light	Very low	Dry iron	Use press cloth on right side.
Acrylic		Moderate		
Cotton	Light to moderate	Moderate to high		Press with dry or steam iron. For more moisture, dampen press cloth or garment and press with dry iron. To avoid shine on dark colours, press from wrong side or use press cloth on right side.
Linen	Light to heavy	High		
Nylon	Light			Little or no ironing required.
Polyester	Moderate			May need press cloth on right side, test first.
Rayon		Low to moderate	Dry or steam iron	Use press cloth to prevent shine and water spots.
Silk	Light			Press light to medium weights with dry iron. For heavyweights, use steam iron and dry press cloth to avoid water spots.
Wool	Light to moderate	Moderate		Press with steam iron. For more moisture, press with dry iron and slightly dampened press cloth on right side to prevent shine. Press crepe with dry iron.
Blends	Press according to requirements of the more delicate fibre.			
Texture				
Crepe	Light	Low to moderate	Dry iron	Use press cloth on right side.
Deep Pile	Finger press	Moderate	Steam iron	See finger pressing above.
Glossy	Light	Low	Dry iron	Use press cloth on right side
Nap, Pile	Light or finger press	Low to moderate	Dry or steam iron	Press fabric over needleboard, using light pressure, or finger press.

VII. Construction

Tailors Ham This is used as a base when pressing curved areas, such as darts and sleeve headings, (a).

Seam Roll This is useful when pressing long curved seams and cylindrical garment sections such as trouser leg seams, (b).

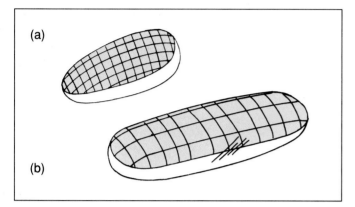

(a)

(b)

Sleeve board This is for pressing narrow garment sections, especially sleeves, that will not fit over a regular ironing board.

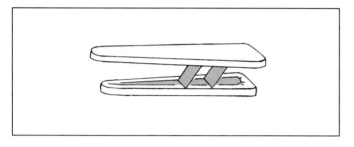

Needleboard This is designed for pressing pile fabrics. The right side is placed face down on the board. As you press the short, dense needles keep the pile from being flattened.

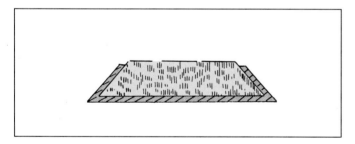

Paper strips These strips should be cut from fairly thick paper. They are placed under seam allowances, the seams are then pressed open. The paper prevents seam allowance imprints on the outside of the garment. These are also used when pressing pleats, see page 41.

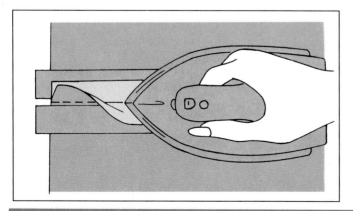

Interfacings

One of the first steps in making a garment is to attach any required interfacing.

Interfacing is an extra layer of fabric that provides shape and support in detail areas of the garment. It is frequently used in collars, cuffs, lapels, necklines, pockets, waistbands and opening edges.

Types of Interfacing

The two basic types of interfacing are sew-in and fusible. Both are available in woven and non-woven versions, in a variety of weights. There are also interfacings suitable for stretch fabrics.

In addition to these specially developed interfacing fabrics, a fine, light linen or cotton, organza or organdie can be used for sheer or lightweight fabrics.

The rule of thumb is that the interfacing should always be slightly lighter in weight than the garment fabric.

Choosing between a fusible or sew-in interfacing is really a matter of personal preference. In general fusibles provide slightly crisper results, are easier to use and, because they bond to the fabric, are excellent for fabrics that fray. However there are a number of fabrics for which they are not suitable. These include heavily textured fabrics,very fine, sheer fabrics and those requiring a cool iron.

The success of these iron-on interfacings is dependent on the correct amount of heat and steam - so do follow the manufacturer's instructions carefully.

Where to Interface

Your pattern will tell you which pieces require interfacing and the back of your pattern envelope will tell you how much to buy.

The interfacing is usually applied to the wrong side of what will ultimately be the outermost layer of the fabric - for example, to the upper collar rather than the under collar, to the cuff rather than to the cuff facing. Since there are exceptions, be sure to follow your pattern instructions.

Cutting and Marking

Woven interfacings have lengthwise, and crosswise grains and bias, just like your garment fabric (see page 15). The interfacing pieces should be cut out so that the pieces are on-grain as indicated in the pattern layouts.

Technically, non-woven interfacings do not have a grain. However, this does not always mean that you can cut out your pieces any old way. Some of these interfacings are stable in all directions, some stretch in the crosswise direction and others are all-bias. Read the instructions that come with the interfacing and follow their recommendations on how to place the pattern pieces.

Because the interfacings are applied at an early stage transfer the pattern markings to the interfacing sections, in addition to the fabric.

Application

Sew-in Type

To minimise bulk, trim the outside corners of the interfacing diagonally just inside the point where your seamlines will meet. Pin the interfacing to the wrong side of the garment section and machine tack 2 mm (1/8") outside the seamline. Trim the interfacing seam allowances close to the stitching and trim off any hem allowances.

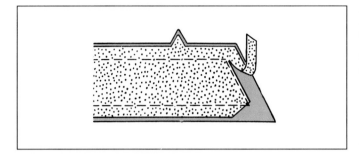

Fusible Type

Cut the interfacing without any seam allowances. On heavy fabrics trim 1 mm (1/16") in from the seamline. Fuse the interfacing in place, following the manufacturer's instructions.

☆ TIP ☆

If the interfacing only partly covers a section of a pattern piece, such as a jacket front or back, avoid a hard line showing on the right side by trimming the interfacing with pinking shears.

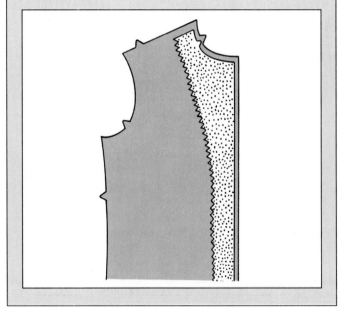

Speciality Interfacings

These have been developed for detail areas such as waistbands, collars, cuffs and plackets. Many of these are pre-cut into the most common widths and some are particularly easy to use because they are perforated to indicate (and reduce bulk on) seamlines and foldlines.

Darts

Darts are one of the ways used to mould the fabric to the curves of the body.

Darts can be straight, for a loose fit, or curved for a tighter fit. They usually start at a seamline and taper to nothing at their tip. However, a double-pointed dart is often used on dresses, jackets and fitted shirts. This is actually two darts in one, and should be sewn as such from the centre to each point. The widest part will be at the waist, and the points at the bust (or shoulder blade) and hips.

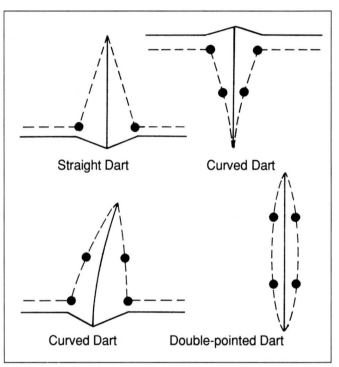

Straight Dart Curved Dart

Curved Dart Double-pointed Dart

Marking a Dart

Examine the shape of your dart. If the stitching line is straight, all you need do is mark the dots.

If the stitching line is curved, it is safest to mark the entire stitching line.

Stitching

1. With right sides together, fold the fabric through the centre of the dart, matching the dots and stitching lines.

2. Place pins at right angles to the stitching line.

3. Stitch the dart from the wide end to the point. To prevent a bubble or poke at the point, make the last few stitches right at the fold and leave the threads long enough to tie a knot. Do **not** back-stitch.

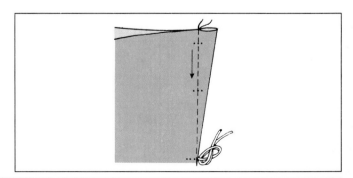

VII. Construction

For double-pointed darts, pin at right angles to the stitching line. Working from the centre stitch to one point then, overlapping for a few stitches, work from the centre again to the other point. Clip into the dart at the widest point so that it will lie flat.

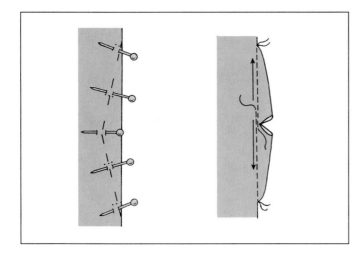

Pressing

Press the darts flat then open or to one side, as your pattern indicates. As a rule vertical darts are pressed toward the centre of the garment and horizontal ones are pressed downward. Occasionally, your pattern instructions will tell you to slash the dart along the foldline, in order to press it open.

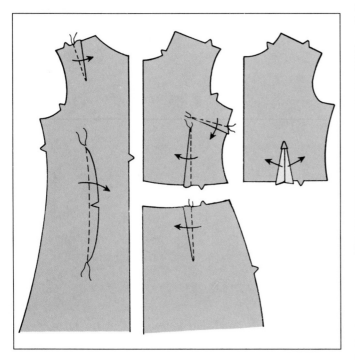

Gathering

Gathers are the simplest means of controlling the fullness of fabric. They are used at waistlines and yokes, cuffs and sleeve heads, on tiers, frills and ruffles. The effect of the gathers will be determined by the fabric. Soft fabric will drape and cling to the body. Crisp fabric will billow out.

You can use hand tacking/basting stitches to create gathers, but the quickest and easiest way is to use a long straight machine stitch.

1. Loosen the needle tension slightly. This will make it easier to pull up the bobbin thread later.

2. Set the stitch length for a long stitch - the heavier the fabric, the longer the stitch.

3. Working on the right side of the fabric and within the seam allowance, stitch just inside the seamline of the area to be gathered. Stitch again 5 mm (1/4") away. Be sure to leave long thread tails. Do **not** back-stitch.

4. With right sides together, pin the section to be gathered to the shorter one, matching notches, seams and markings.

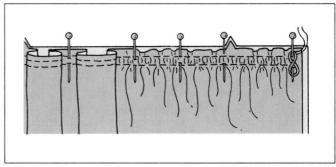

5. Gently pull the bobbin threads at each end, sliding the fabric along until it fits the shorter section. At both ends, wrap the excess bobbin thread around the pins in a figure of eight. Distribute the gathers evenly and pin as shown.

6. Re-adjust your machine stitch length and tension, and working with the gathered side up, stitch along the seamline.

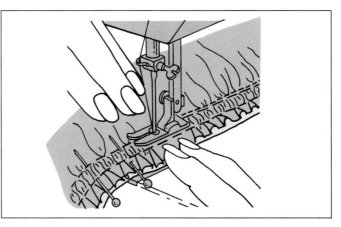

Gathering Long Sections

The longer the area you are working on, the greater the risk of a thread breaking while you pull up the gathers. To avoid this divide the length into equal parts to be gathered and mark with pins.

Machine separate rows of gathering stitches for each section.

Gathering Over a Cord

This is a fast method for gathering long sections without the problem of threads breaking.

1. Cut a piece of strong thin cord, such as pearl cotton, button and carpet thread, or lightweight packing string, slightly longer than the edge to be gathered.

If the gathers intersect a seam on light or mediumweight fabrics, diagonally trim the ends of the seam allowances before stitching the gathers.

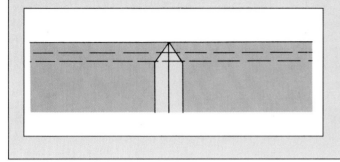

If the gathers intersect a seam on bulky fabrics, trim the ends of the seams and stitch up to the seams, keeping the seam allowances free.

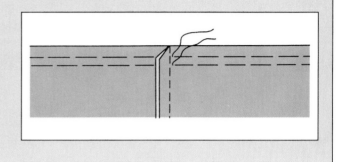

2. Set your machine for a zig-zag stitch wide enough to stitch over the cord without catching it in the stitches. Position the cord within the seam allowance and place under the machine presser foot so that the left swing of the needle falls just short of the seamline, stitch across the area to be gathered.

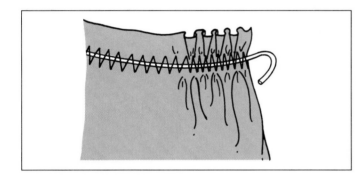

3. Secure one end of the cord.

4. Pin the two sections together, matching notches, seamlines and markings. To distribute the gathers, hold the cord taut, and slide the fabric along it.

5. Re-set the machine to straight stitching. Working with the gathered side up, stitch along the seamline, being careful not to catch the cord. Depending on the weight of your fabric and the thickness of your cord, you may find it easier to use your machine's zipper foot.

6. When you have finished stitching just pull out the cord.

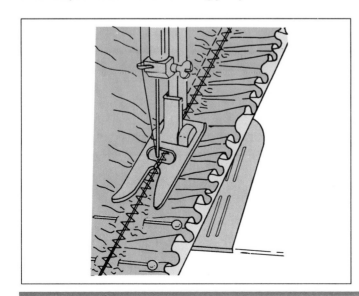

Shirring Elastic

This is often used to decorative effect on the yokes of children's dresses as well as cuff and neck edges. It can also be further enhanced with smocking stitches. Shirring elastic can be easily applied with your sewing machine.

1. Wind the shirring elastic by hand on to the bobbin and use your normal thread (or a nylon thread) on top.

2. Using a long stitch, apply with parallel rows of stitches on the wrong side of the garment. With every row the fabric will gather more.

3. Gently pull up the elastic thread to increase the gathers further.

4. Catch and secure all the thread ends in the side seams.

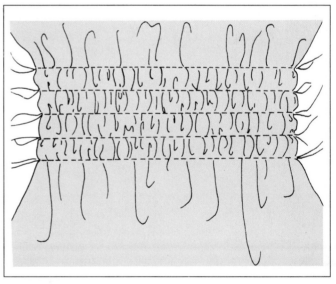

Smocking

Smocked fabrics have a series of folds decoratively stitched together on the right side. A series of dots, aligned with the grain of the fabric are transferred to the fabric as a stitching guide. Stitches are worked from left to right.

VII. Construction

Cable Stitch

1. At A bring the needle to the right side, then keeping the thread above the needle, take a small stitch at B, draw up fabric.

2. Keeping the thread below the needle, take a small stitch at C, draw up fabric.

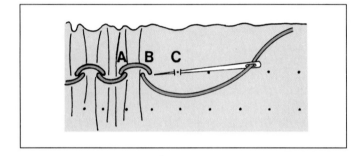

3. Continue alternating the thread above and below the needle, taking care to pull the thread at right angles to the stitch to ensure the folds are even.

Honeycomb Stitch

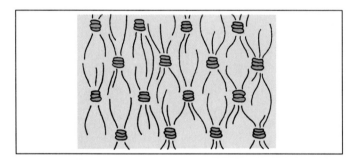

1. Bring the needle to right side at A, take a small stitch at B, then another at A, pull the thread taut.

2. Re-insert the needle at B, and bring it up one row below at C, take a small stitch at D, then another at C, pull thread taut.

3. Re-insert the needle at D, and out at E, continue alternating from row to row.

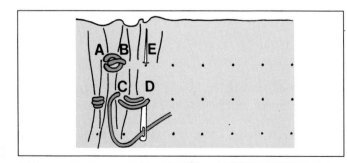

Diamond Stitch

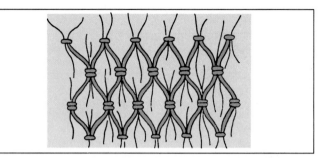

1. At A bring the needle to the right side, then keeping the thread above the needle, take a small stitch at B, draw up fabric.

2. Take a small stitch one row below at C, then keeping the thread below the needle, take a small stitch at D, draw up fabric.

3. Return to the first row and take a small stitch at E.

4. Continue to alternate from row to row, with the thread above the needle on upper rows and below the needle on lower rows.

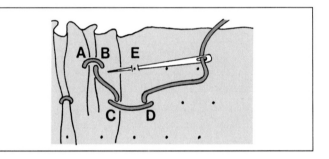

Pleats

Pleats require accurate cutting, marking and sewing. If you are as much as 1-2 mm (1/16" to 1/8") out on each pleat this can add up to 2 to 3 cm (1" to 1 1/2") on the finished waist measurement. Marking pleat foldlines with thread is the most accurate, as the thickness of crayon can be misleading and tracing paper is sometimes difficult to handle accurately.

Mark the pleats on the wrong side of the material, then transfer the marks to the right side if necessary. Mark both the foldlines and the placement lines. Whichever method of marking you are using, use a different colour for each these so that you can quickly distinguish between the lines.

Knife or Straight Pleats

These pleats all face in the same direction.

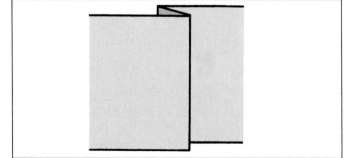

1. Fold the fabric on the foldline and bring the fold to the placement line following the arrows printed on the pattern piece.

2. Pin or tack/baste the pleats along the folded edges, then tack/baste across the top of all the pleats.

3. If the pleats are to be pressed, do it before the pleated section is attached to the rest of the garment.

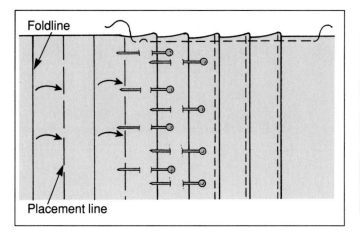

can make the cutting layout easier and also help when matching plaids or stripes. If the underlay is part of the garment section tack/baste the two foldlines together. Then spread open the underfold and match the foldline to the placement line and press. Tack/baste across the top of the pleat.

If the inverted pleat has a separate underlay section, the two garment pieces are tacked/basted together along the foldlines. Press the seam open, then seam the underlay to the garment.

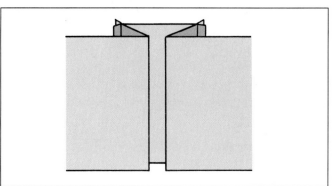

Box Pleats

Each pleat consists of two straight pleats facing opposite directions with the centre part on the right side. Fold, tack/baste and press as for straight pleats.

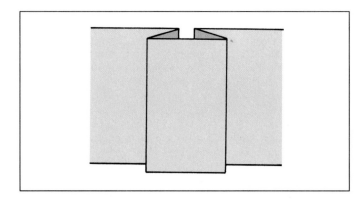

Inverted Pleats

These are the opposite of box pleats and are often used at the centre front or back.

The main difference between an inverted pleat and a box pleat is that an inverted pleat does not have to be cut out of one piece of material. Being able to cut the underlay separately

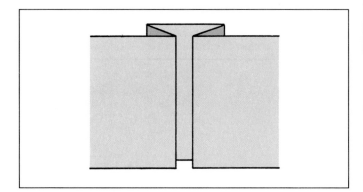

Pressing

The best looking pleats are those that have been carefully and properly pressed.

For soft (unpressed) pleats

Use a dry pressing cloth. Hold the iron 5 to 7 cm (2" to 3") above the fabric and apply steam only. Do **not** press the iron directly on the fabric.

For crisp firmly pressed pleats

Once the pleats are formed, you will be pressing over several thicknesses of fabric. As you do not want these layers to create ridges on the outside of your garment, always use a pressing cloth. If you have not got one, use a linen tea cloth.

Before removing the tacking/basting stitches press the pleats **very lightly** to establish the fold line. Remove the tacking/basting stitches as they might leave marks when pressing firmly. Put strips of brown paper between the garment and the untacked/unbasted fold of each pleat.

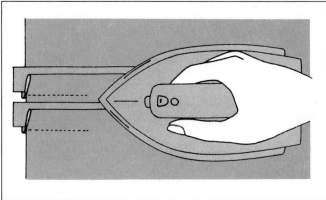

Fabric permitting, use a damp cloth, plenty of steam, and the full pressure of your iron. It is advisable to check the heat, steam and pressure of the iron on a small piece of the material before starting. Since the garment still has to be hemmed, press **lightly** within the area 20 cm (8") above the hemline. Then re-press thoroughly once the hem is made.

Once you have pressed the pleats, be sure your garment is thoroughly dry before handling it.

VII. Construction

Top-stitching and Edge-stitching

Pleats are often top-stitched and/or edge-stitched to hold them in place. The top-stitching, which starts at the waistline and extends to the hip area, is done through all the layers.

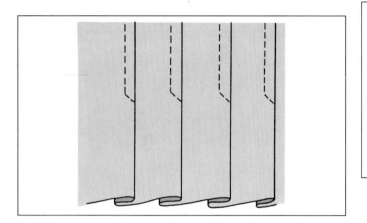

If the fabric does not hold a crease well, it is also a good idea to edge-stitch below the hip, catching only the fold of the pleat in your stitching. If you are going to wash the garment rather than have it dry cleaned, edge-stitching will also make the pleats much easier to re-press.

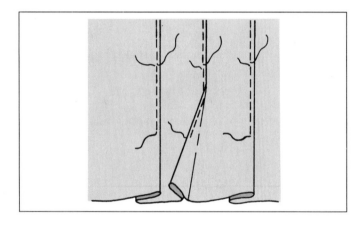

To make the top-stitching and edge-stitching look like one continuous line, edge-stitch the pleat fold below the hip-line first. Edge-stitch to within 20 cm (8") of the hemline. Then, starting at the waistline edge, top-stitch between the waist and the hip, overlapping the stitches at the hip-line. Once the garment is hemmed, go back and complete the edge-stitching.

Hemming

Where a seam falls at the inside fold of a pleat, to make the hem less bulky, clip the seam allowance to the line of stitching at the top of the hem allowance. Press the seam open below

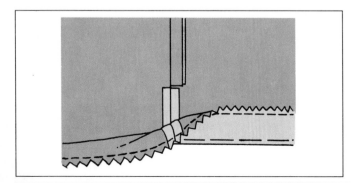

the clip and trim to 5 mm (1/4"). Finish the raw edge of the hem and sew in place, (see Hems on page 47).

Finally, on the inside of the garment, edge-stitch the pleat fold within the hem allowance.

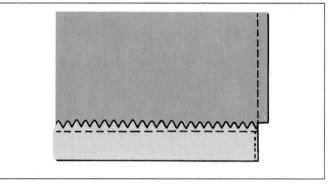

Facings

A facing is a piece of fabric that finishes a garment edge. Facings are most frequently found at necklines, armholes, front and back openings and, occasionally at the waistline or the lower edge of a sleeve.

Most facings are created by attaching a separate piece of fabric to the garment edge. However there are times when it is better to include the facing in with the original piece of material. This can only be done if the finished edge at that point lays on the straight grain of the fabric. It is then possible to cut the extra material in one piece with the main part. This is known as a self-facing or extension.

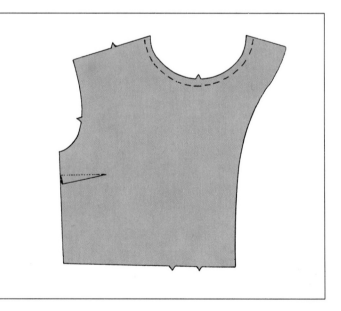

Although the shape and the location can vary, the basics for creating a facing that lays flat and looks professional remain the same.

Interface

First apply interfacing, to either the facing section or the garment section, as required, (see Interfacings on page 36).

Finish the edge

Stitch the facing pieces together at the shoulder or side seams, then neaten the outer edge, (see Seam Finishes on page 33).

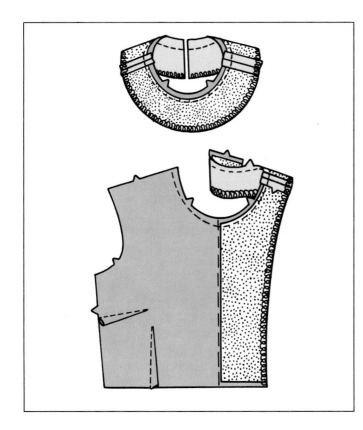

Attach the facing

With right sides together, stitch the facing to the garment as indicated on your pattern instructions. If there are any corners, remember to shorten your stitch length for about 2.5 cm (1") on either side, (see Corners on page 32).

Trim and grade

To prevent ridges from showing on the outside, remove bulk from the seams by trimming the seam allowances to 5 mm (1/4"). On thick fabrics, also trim the facing seam allowance to 3 mm (1/8") so that the layers are graded. To ensure a smooth edge when the facing is turned to the inside, clip or notch curved seam allowances, (see Trimming and Clipping on page 34).

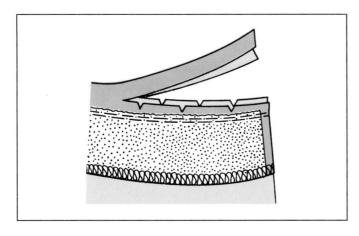

Press

Press the seam allowances flat to blend the stitches. Next, press them open. Then press them toward the facing.

Under-stitch

To stop the facing and the seam rolling to the right side of the garment, open the facing out. With the facing on the top, stitch through the facing and both seam allowances very close to the seam, as shown (also see page 26).

If you have clipped the curves, under-stitch carefully, checking frequently to make sure those small wedges of seam allowance do not get caught in the stitching.

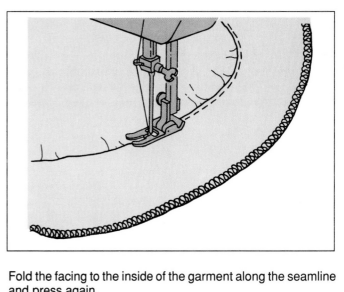

Fold the facing to the inside of the garment along the seamline and press again.

To keep the facing in place, secure it at the seamlines only by (a) whip stitching, (b) stitching in the seam groove or (c) using a small piece of fusible webbing.

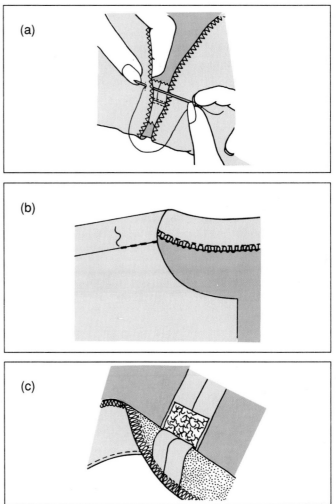

VII. Construction

Bindings

Bindings make a decorative edge and are an alternative to facings.

On sheer fabrics, narrow self-fabric bindings eliminate the problem of unsightly facings showing through.

Bindings can be made in contrasting fabric as a design feature.

Bindings are an easy and neat way to finish the edges on reversible garments.

Bindings are often used as edgings in home furnishings, such as place-mats, curtains, tablecloths and quilts.

If you are adding binding to a pattern that does not feature it, or using binding instead of a facing, remember that no seam allowance will be required on the edges to be bound.

For flexibility, bindings are cut on the bias. Decide on the width of the bias binding you require and either purchase the required length or make your own.

Making Your Own Binding

Continuous Method

1. Cut a rectangle of the fabric you are going to use. The longer side of the rectangle can follow either the lengthwise or the widthwise grain of your fabric. Trim each side of the rectangle so that it **exactly** follows a thread of the fabric.

2. Fold one corner of the rectangle so that the widthwise and the lengthwise edges meet; press the fold, then open out the rectangle. (The crease is the true bias).

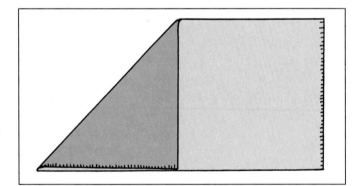

3. Cut a cardboard template the width required for your bias strips. Each strip should be four times the width of the finished binding. For example, for a 5 mm (¼") finished binding width, mark 2 cm (1") wide strips; for a 1.5 cm (½") binding mark 6 cm (2") wide strips. 4. With the wrong side of the material facing up and using the crease as your starting point, and the cardboard template as your guide, mark parallel diagonal lines across the width of the fabric.

5. Cut off the two triangles at opposite corners of the rectangle.

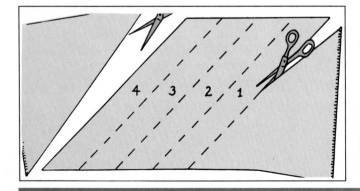

6. With right sides together, fold the fabric into a tube matching the lines so that one width of binding extends beyond the edge at each end of the tube. Sew a 5 mm (¼") seam, press open.

7. Starting at one end, cut along the marked line, working your way around the tube until you have separated it into one long continuous strip.

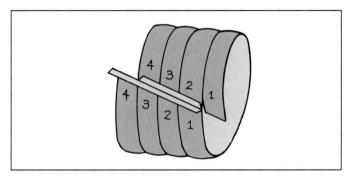

Joining individual bias strips

1. Using bias-cut strips the required width and with right sides together, pin the end of the strips so that they form a 90 degree angle. Stitch a 5 mm (¼") seam.

2. Press the seam open and trim away the points that extend beyond the edge of the binding.

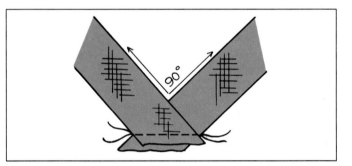

Attaching Your Own Binding or Double Fold Bias Tape

Because it is the fastest method, many patterns tell you to apply the binding entirely by machine. However, the following combination of machine and hand sewing is easier and although it may take a few minutes longer, that extra time will pay off in results.

When applying 2 cm (1") wide bias strips use 5 mm (¼") wide seams, for 4 cm (1½") wide strips use 1 cm (⅜") wide seams.

When applying double fold bias tape, open it out and follow the foldlines for your seam widths.

On binding that you have made yourself, fold and press under on one long edge before you begin. The fold should be equal to one quarter of the width of the binding. This will give you the folded edge you need for step 2.

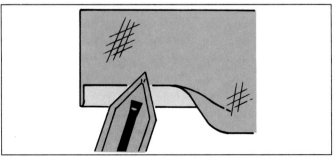

1. With right sides together and matching raw edges, pin then machine stitch the binding to the garment edge.

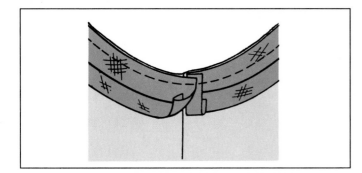

2. Turn the folded edge of the binding to the inside so that it encases the raw edge and just covers the stitching line; slip-stitch in place.

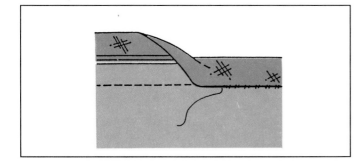

At an outward corner

1. Before you begin, use a fabric marking pen, dressmakers pencil or tailors chalk to mark where the seam allowances intersect at the corner.

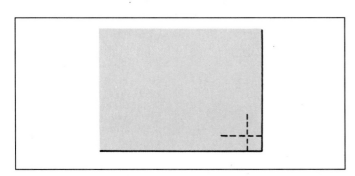

2. Follow step 1 for Attaching Your Own Binding, end your stitching where the seamlines intersect at the corner. Back-stitch one or two stitches and cut the thread.

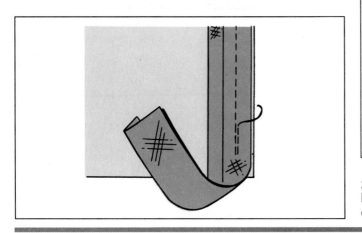

3. Fold the binding back on itself to create a diagonal crease at the corner. Then fold it back again so that this new fold is in line with the edge of the binding on side A (see diagram below) and the seamlines of the binding match on side B.

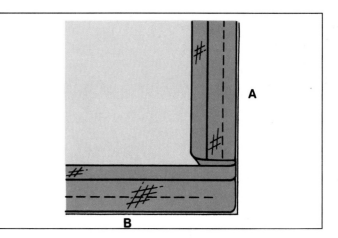

4. Insert the needle exactly at the corner marking and continue stitching.

5. Finish according to step 2 for Attaching Your Own Binding, making a diagonal fold at the corner. If desired, slip-stitch the corner folds also.

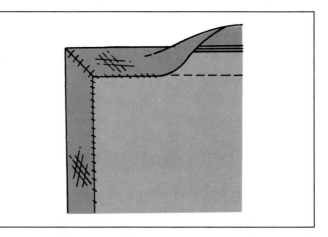

At an inward corner

1. Reinforce the corner with small stitches along the seamline. Clip the corner just to the stitches.

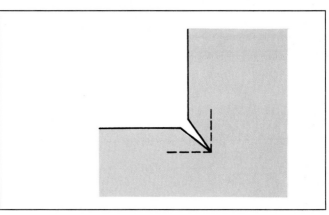

2. Following step 1 for Attaching Your Own Binding, stitch binding to one fabric edge. Stop stitching when you reach the corner.

VII. Construction

3. Keeping the needle in the fabric, raise the presser foot and spread the fabric open at the clip so that it lines up with the edge of the binding. Lower the presser foot and continue stitching.

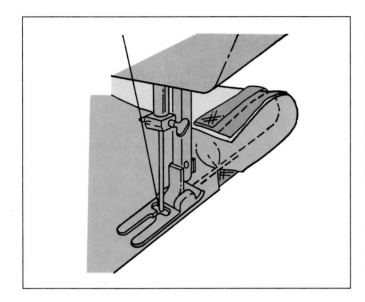

4. Press the seam allowances towards the binding. As you do this, a diagonal fold will form at the corner.

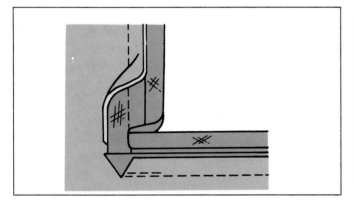

☆ TIP ☆

Be careful not to stretch the binding as you sew, particularly when you are working on a curved edge. You may find it helpful to use steam to pre-shape the binding before you apply it.

Pin the binding to your ironing board in a curve that matches the shape of the garment edge. Using a generous amount of steam, shrink out the excess fullness, let the binding dry, then attach it to the garment

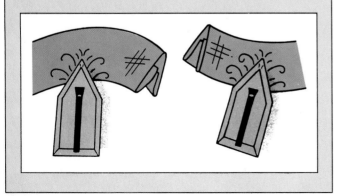

5. Finish according to step 2 for Attaching Your Own Binding, forming another diagonal fold at the corner. If desired, slip-stitch the corner folds.

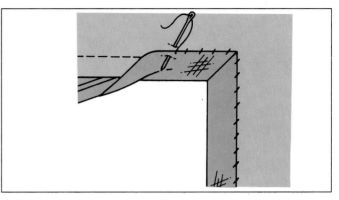

Edge-stitched Application

This method is for purchased double fold bias binding or fold-over braid. These braids are folded so that one side is slightly wider than the other.

1. Slip the binding over the raw garment edge with the wider side of the tape covering the wrong side of the fabric.

2. Then working with the right side uppermost, edge-stitch the tape in place, through all layers of fabric.

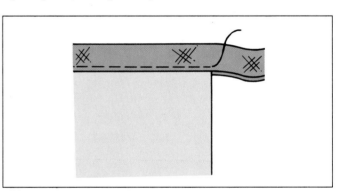

At an outward corner

1. Edge-stitch the binding all the way to the raw edge of the fabric. Remove the fabric from the machine and cut the threads.

2. Turn the binding around the corner and down the next side; pin.

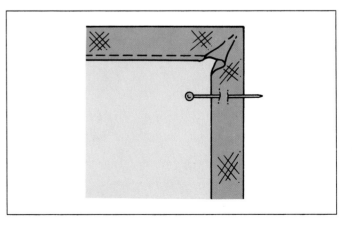

3. Make a diagonal fold on both sides of the corner; press.

4. Beginning just below the diagonal fold, back-stitch to the fold, then edge-stitch along the binding. If desired, slip-stitch the corner folds.

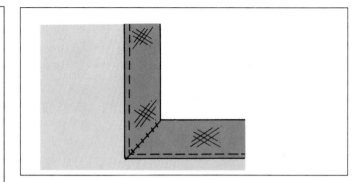

4. Press the binding at the corner so that a diagonal fold forms on both sides of the garment. If desired, slip-stitch the corner folds to keep them in place.

At an inward corner

1. Reinforce the corner with small machine stitches. Clip the corner just to the stitches.
2. Edge-stitch the binding to the garment, stopping at the corner.

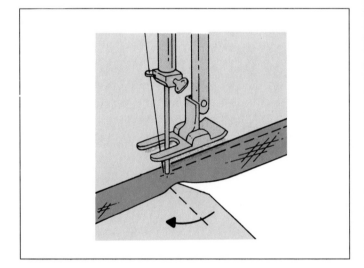

3. Keeping the needle in the fabric, raise the presser foot and spread the fabric to straighten the garment edge. Slip the binding over the fabric, lower the presser foot, and continue edge-stitching.

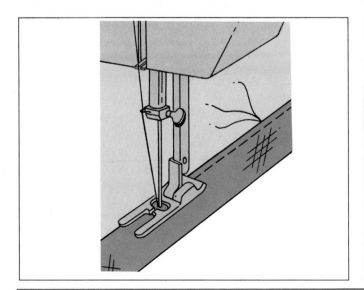

☆ TIP ☆

Begin and end the binding at an inconspicuous seam, such as the centre back or underarm. Press under one end of the binding. As you machine stitch for step 1, lap the pressed end over the unpressed end.

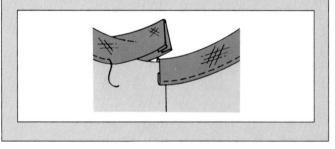

Hems

Hems can be sewn by hand or machine, or simply fused in place, (see page 49). If you hand sew, your stitches should be invisible on the right side, (see Hand Hemming Stitches on page 28).

Prior to hemming a dress, skirt or coat, it is advisable to let the garment hang for 24 hours to let it settle. This is especially important for heavier fabrics or jerseys which can drop and also on full skirts where part of the skirt hangs on the bias.

Try on the garment wearing the appropriate underclothes and accessories (especially shoes) before marking the desired hemline, as this can influence your decision.

If possible enlist a friend to help you determine the most flattering length and ensure it is level.

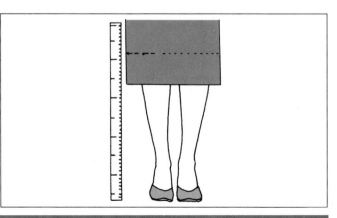

VII. Construction

Stand still with your feet together and ask a friend to measure up from the floor and mark the hemline with pins. These should be inserted parallel to the floor and about 5 cm (2") apart.

Turn the hem up along the pin-marked line and, matching seamlines, pin in place close to the foldline. Also pin every 5 cm (2") at right angles to the hem edge to hold the hem allowance in place. Try the garment on again.

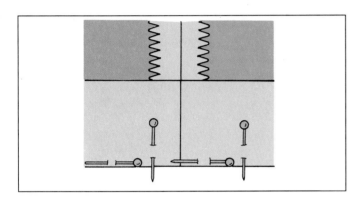

Unless making a machine-rolled hem or narrow top-stitched hem, tack/baste close to the foldline removing all pins and press.

Trimming

Measure and mark the desired hem allowance plus 5 mm (1/4") extra for finishing. Trim away the excess. The type of hem you choose as well as the shape of the hemline, will determine the depth of the hem allowance. On a straight garment, the hem allowance should be from 5 to 7.5 cm (2" to 3"). On an A-line or flared garment, the hem allowance is usually between 4 and 5 cm (1 1/2" to 2").

☆ TIP ☆

If your fabric is bulky, trim away any seam allowances, between the lower edge and the hemline, to 5 mm (1/4").

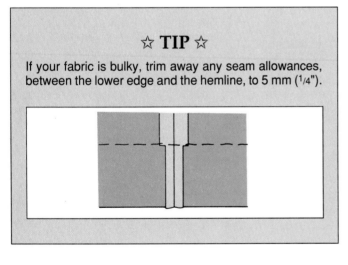

Easing

If the garment edge is slightly curved, the hem allowance will have extra fullness. Unless this fullness is eased so that the hem allowance lies flat against the garment, your finished hem will have ripples and ridges.

Easing is done after the hem allowance is trimmed, but before the raw edge is finished.

1. Ease-stitch 5 mm (1/4") from the edge, remembering to loosen the needle tension slightly.

2. Working on a flat surface, use a pin to draw up the thread to ease the extra fullness.

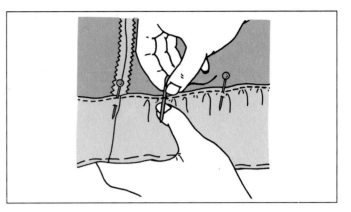

3. Steam press to shrink out some of the fullness.

Hand Sewn Hems

If your fabric does not fray, you do not need to finish the edge. If finishing **is** necessary, either the over sewn, stitched and pinked, zig-zag, or turned and stitched seam finishes described on pages 27 and 33 would be suitable. Alternatively use a seam binding. To apply this, lap the binding 5 mm (1/4") over the hem edge and edge-stitch in place, (see pages 34 and 46). Now, depending on your choice of fabric, hand hem stitch in place, (see Hand Hemming Stitches on page 28).

Machine Stitched Hems

These are the quick and easy solution. Your machine may have a number of built in stitches, such as a blind-hemming stitch, and you should refer to your manual for details of these.

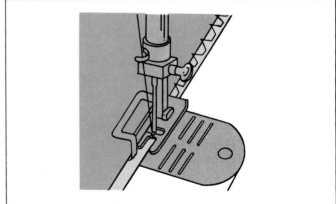

Narrow Top-stitched Hem

This finish is suitable for sheer, lightweight or mediumweight fabrics.

1. Press the hem up along the hemline, then trim the allowance to 2.5 cm (1"). Fold the raw edge in to meet the first crease and press again.

2. Working on the right side, top-stitch close to the inner edge of the hem allowance.

3. If desired, top-stitch again close to the hemline.

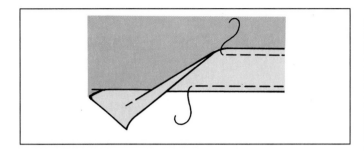

Wide Top-stitched Hem

This technique can be used on all fabrics and styles, except for very curved hems. If the hem is slightly curved, be sure to ease-stitch it before top-stitching.

For the most attractive proportions, the hem allowance should be 4 to 5 cm (1½" to 2") deep.

1. Press the hem up along the hemline. Ease in the fullness on any curves.

2. For woven fabrics, first press the raw edge under 1.5 cm (½"), for knits leave edge unfinished.

3. Working on the wrong side, stitch close to the edge of the hem allowance.

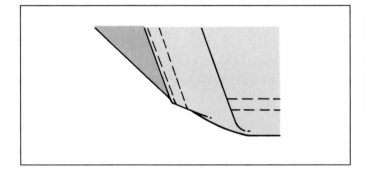

Machine-rolled Hem

This is a quick and easy way to achieve the narrow rolled hem look that is right for sheers, lightweight silk and synthetic fabrics, and for hemming frills and ruffles.

Note: Your garment needs a minimum hem allowance of 1.5 cm (½").

1. Mark the hemline 3 mm (⅛") longer than desired. Fold the garment up along this hemline then stitch close to the fold. Do not press before you stitch, if the hemline is not on a straight grain, pressing first will distort the hem.

2. Using embroidery scissors, carefully trim away the hem allowance above the stitching.

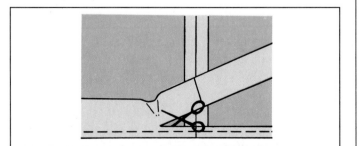

3. Fold the hem allowance up along the stitching line, rolling the stitching line just slightly to the inside of the garment; press.

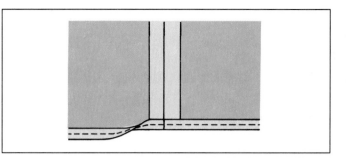

4. Stitch again close to the inner fold; press.

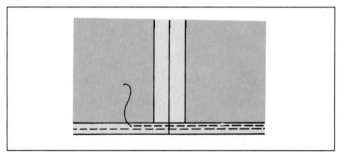

☆ TIP ☆

When making the machine-rolled hem on sheers, use long tacking/basting stitches for the first row of stitching, then remove them when the hem is completed.

Fused Hems

This no-sew method of hemming is suitable for all but very sheer or lightweight fabrics. Fusible web is packaged in pre-cut strips or on rolls.

The strip of web should be narrower than the hem allowance. Sandwich the strip between the hem allowance and the garment, just below the finished edge. Fuse in place following the manufacturer's instructions.

To make sure no ridges appear on the right side of the garment, test the fusible web on scraps first. If ridges show, pink the edges of the web before applying and try not to rest the iron on the finished edge of the hem allowance.

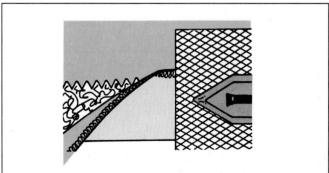

VII. Construction

Mitres

When an edge is folded in at a corner fullness is created at the inside edge of the fabric. The excess is most tidily disposed of by forming a mitre.

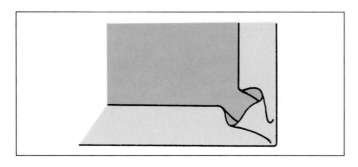

Bindings require a slightly different technique, because they encase the edge of the fabric, (see Bindings on page 44).

Folded Mitre

This method works for patch pockets.

1. Stitch along the pocket seamlines, then press the seam allowances to the inside along the stitching lines.

2. Open out the seam allowances at the corners. Fold the corner up diagonally and press, then trim this seam allowance to 5 mm ($1/4$").

3. Fold all seam allowances back to the inside. The folded edges will just meet, forming a neat corner.

4. To make sure the corners stay neat slip-stitch them together. For pockets that are to be edge-stitched or top-stitched in position, the corners could be secured with fusible web.

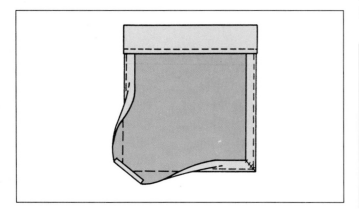

Stitched Mitre

1. Turn the edges, where the mitre is to be formed to the inside along the seamlines or foldlines; press.

2. Open out the pressed edges. Fold the corner diagonally across the point so that the pressed lines meet; press.

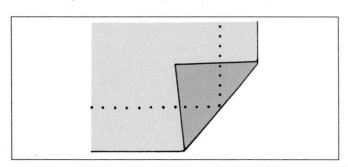

3. Open out the corner and with right sides together, fold the garment diagonally through the corner so that the creases meet as shown. Stitch along the diagonal crease line.

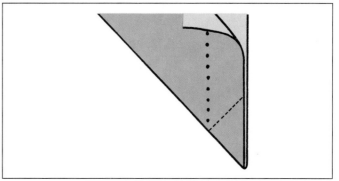

4. Trim the corner seam allowance, trimming diagonally at the point. Press the corner seam open.

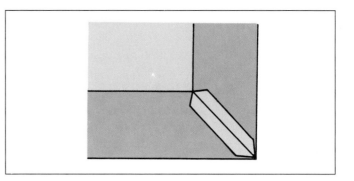

5. Turn the seam allowances or hem facing to the inside and press.

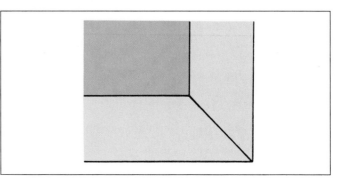

Flat Trims

Flat trims also need to be mitred when they turn a corner. The style of trim, for example, whether it has two straight edges or one straight edge and one decorative edge, determines which technique is to be used.

If the trim is to be anywhere except along the edge of the garment, mark the trim placement line so that it is visible on the outside of the garment.

For trims with two straight edges

Note: With this technique, the right edge of the trim is aligned with the garment edge, or the placement line.

1. Pin the trim to the garment edge or along the placement line. Top-stitch both edges, ending the stitching when you reach the corner.

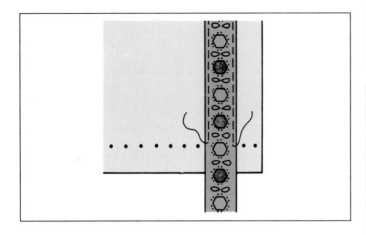

2. Fold the trim back on itself and press. Then fold the trim diagonally so that it meets the intersecting garment edge or placement line, press to form a crease line.

3. Re-fold the trim back up on itself and stitch along the diagonal crease through all the layers.

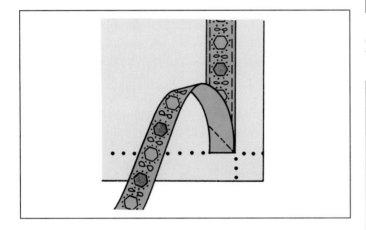

4. Fold the trim back down so that it meets the intersecting garment edge or the placement line again and press. Then continue top-stitching along both edges of the trim.

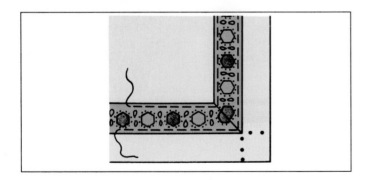

For trims with one straight edge and one decorative edge

Note: For this technique, the left (straight) edge of the trim is aligned with the garment edge or placement line.

1. Pin the straight edge of the trim to the garment edge or along the placement line. Top-stitch all the way to the corner.

2. Working at your ironing board, fold the trim back up on itself, positioning the fold slightly below the garment edge or placement line. Then fold the trim back down so that it meets the intersecting garment edge or placement line. Secure the trim to your ironing board with a few straight pins, press the corner.

Note: You may have to re-fold the trim several times until you get it just right and are ready to press.

3. Re-fold the trim back up on itself and stitch along the diagonal crease through all layers.

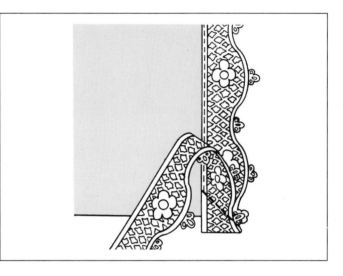

4. Open out the trim, press again and continue stitching the trim to the garment.

VIII. Collars and Bands

Collars

Generally, collars are made up of two layers of garment fabric forming a top collar and an under collar with a layer of interfacing sandwiched between.

There are many different styles of collar but in construction they fall into three basic categories.

Flat Collar

This lies flat against the garment. Compare the neck edges of the garment and collar and the curves will be almost identical.

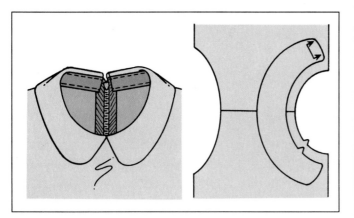

Rolled Collar

This stands up from the neck edge then rolls down to rest on the garment. The curve of a roll collar is less than the curve of the neck edge of the garment.

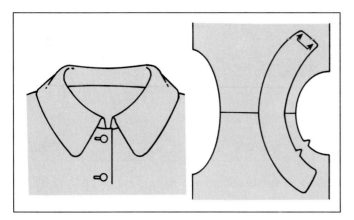

Standing Collar

This collar stands straight up from the neckline. The collar is very straight compared to the neckline curve.

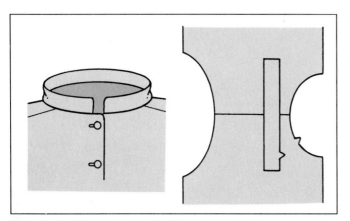

Interfacing

Generally, you would use your collar pattern piece as a guide for cutting the interfacing.

On fusible interfacings, do not add seam allowance. On non-fusibles, tack the interfacing in place and trim and grade the seam allowances **after** stitching, (see Interfacings on page 36).

Stitching

With right sides together, pin the collar and the under collar together, then stitch.

A good way of ensuring an even and symmetrical line to your collar is to stitch it in two steps. Beginning at the centre back stitch first to one edge and then, overlapping several stitches, to the other.

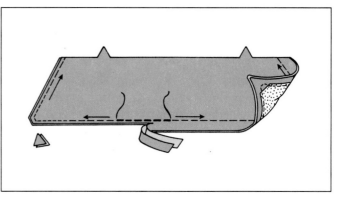

Trimming and Grading

Trim the seam allowances and snip across the corners. On medium and heavyweight fabrics, grade the seam allowances so that the undercollar seam allowance is narrower than the upper collar seam allowance. Notch curved edges, (see page 34).

Pressing

Before turning the collar right side out, press it flat on both sides to blend the stitches, then press the turnings open.

Turn the collar right side out, and using a blunt point such as a knitting needle (not sharp scissor tips), coax out the collar points.

Press the collar flat rolling the seamline slightly to the under side of the collar.

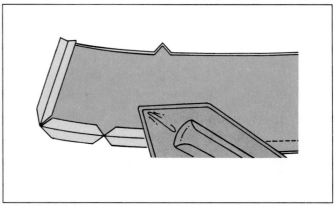

Under-stitching

This is helps keep the undercollar from rolling to the outside.

1. Turn the collar inside out again and slip it under your presser foot so that the right side of the undercollar is facing you.

2. Stitch on the undercollar next to the seamline, catching all the seam allowances in your stitching.

Note: If your collar is curved, you will be able to under-stitch along the entire length of the collar. If your collar is pointed, under-stitch along the back edge, between, and almost to, the points.

3. Turn the collar right side out and press again.

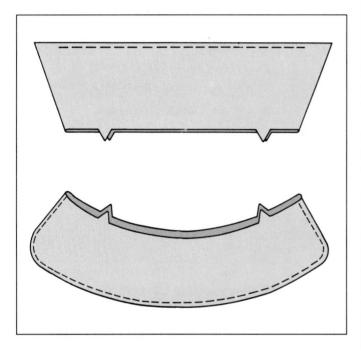

Before Attaching the Collar

1. Always stay-stitch (see page 25) the garment neck edge to prevent it from stretching as you sew.

2. Clip the neckline seam allowance at regular intervals to within 5 mm (1/4") of the stay-stitching. This helps it to lay flat as you stitch the collar in place.

3. Trim, grade and clip your neck edge seam allowances.

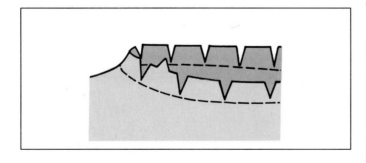

Attaching the Collar

There are different methods for attaching a collar, depending on the type of collar and whether facings are used or not. Sometimes it is attached at the same time as the neckline facing so that the facing hides the seam allowances. If there is no facing, the collar will encase the seam allowances.

To attach a collar with a facing

1. Pin the right side of the under collar to the right side of the garment, matching seams and notches.

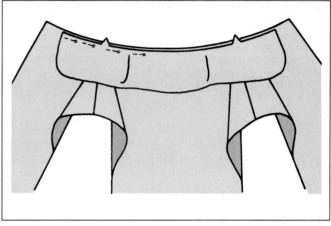

2. Then attach the right side of the facing to the upper collar.

3. Stitch through all thicknesses (facing, upper collar, under-collar and garment). Trim, grade and clip seam allowances.

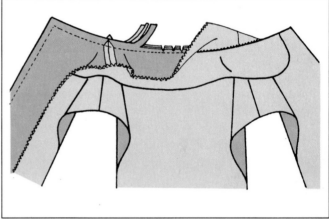

4. Press the seam flat to blend the stitches, then press it open between the facing and the collar seam allowances.

5. Press the seam allowances towards the facing.

6. On the right side of the garment, understitch 2 mm (1/8") from the seamline, through the facing and the seam allowances.

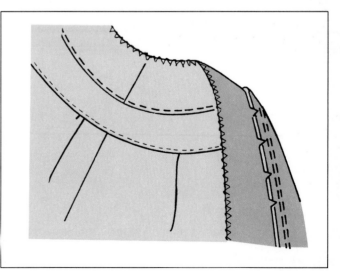

VIII. Collars and Bands

7. Press the facing to the inside of the garment and whip stitch (see page 28) in place at seamlines.

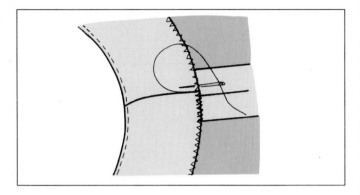

To attach a standing collar

1. Turn under the neck seam allowance of the collar facing and press.

2. Pin the right side of the collar to the right side of the garment, matching seams and notches.

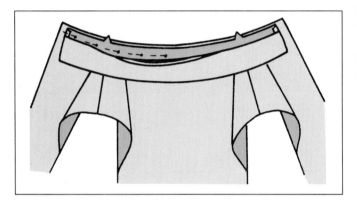

3. Stitch along the seamline, taking care not to catch the collar facing in the stitching.

4. Trim, grade and notch the seam allowances.

5. Press the seam flat to blend the stitches, then press the seam allowances towards the collar.

6. Bring the seam allowances of the collar facing down to the neck seamline. Pin in place, then slip-stitch to the garment.

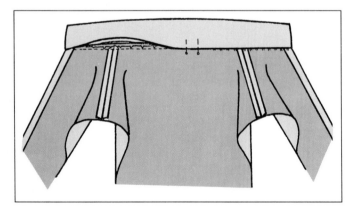

Shirt Collar on a Stand

This type of collar is found on men's shirts and consists of two parts, the stand and the collar, which are sometimes two pieces, sometimes all in one.

If the collar and stand are in one piece make up as given for the standing collar.

If the collar has separate collar and stand sections the following method is used.

1. Interface, stitch, trim, grade, notch and press the collar section as described before.

2. Edge-stitch or top-stitch, as required.

3. Interface the wrong side of the collar stand.

4. Turn the neck seam allowance of the stand facing up towards the wrong side of the facing. Tack/baste in place, then press.

5. With right sides together and matching notches, pin the lower edge of the under collar to the stand and the stand facing to the upper collar. Stitch through all thicknesses.

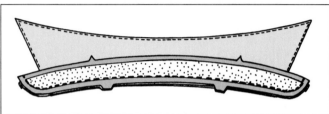

6. Press the seam flat. Then trim, grade, notch and clip the seam allowances.

7. Press the seam open, then down towards the stand.

8. Pin the right side of the collar stand to the right side of the garment, matching seams and notches.

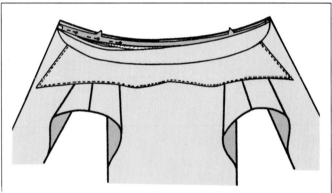

9. Stitch along the seamline. Trim, grade and notch the seam allowances.

10. Press the seam flat to blend the stitches, then press the seam allowances towards the collar. Bring the seam allowances of the stand facing down to the neck seamline.

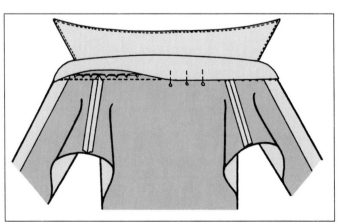

11. Pin in place, then slip-stitch to the garment.

Bands

Bands are a neat and decorative way to finish necklines and front closings (also see Bindings on page 44).

Lapped V-necked Band

This type of band is popular on knitted pull-on tops. It can be made from matching or contrasting stretch or bias cut fabric.

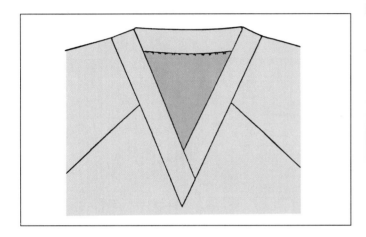

1. On the garment front, reinforce the 'V' at the point of the neckline with a row of small machine stitches just inside the seam allowance.

2. With right sides together and beginning on side A of the garment, pin the band to the neck edge, matching the markings. Leave the end of the band free on side B.

3. Stitch from the point of the 'V' on side A to the last marking on side B of the band. Tie the thread ends.

4. Clip the garment seam allowance to the piont of the 'V' taking care not to cut the reinforcement stitching.

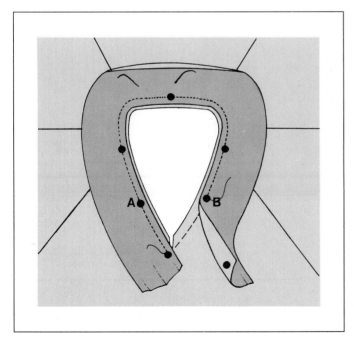

5. Fold the band in half and then the unstitched seam allowance of the band up towards the fold.

6. Tuck the end of side A to the wrong side of the garment. Pin the band over the seam allowances on side A.

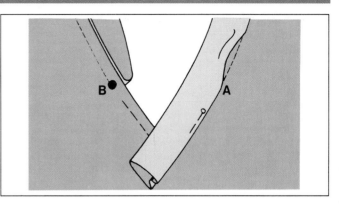

7. Tuck side B to the wrong side and lap over side A. Tack/baste in place.

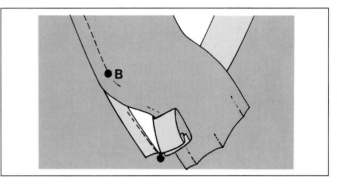

8. With garment side up, stitch the remainder of the seam on side B of the neckline through all thicknesses, ending the stitching at the point of the 'V'. Tie the thread ends.

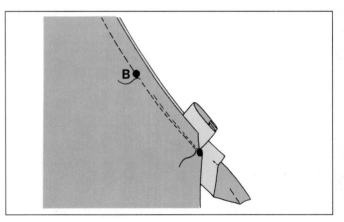

9. Turn under the ends of B, fold the remainder of the band over the seam allowance, enclosing the end of side A and slip-stitch in place.

10. Slip-stitch the loose end of the band B to the seamed edge of A.

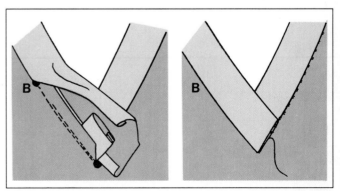

VIII. Collars and Bands

Placket Band

This type of band is often used on shirts and dresses and can be a functional opening as well as a decorative finish. For women the traditional crossing is right over left, for men's or unisex garments it is left over right.

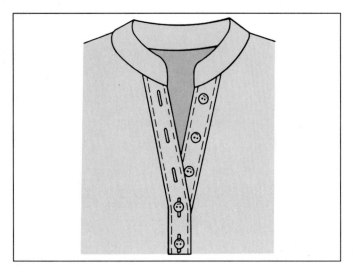

Make sure **all** the markings, including stitching lines, and foldlines are transfered to the garment and band sections.

Note: the following instructions are for a right over left crossing.

1. Reinforce the opening along the stitching line with small machine stitches.

2. Slash between the rows of stitching to within 1 cm (1/2") of stitching at bottom, then carefully clip into the corners.

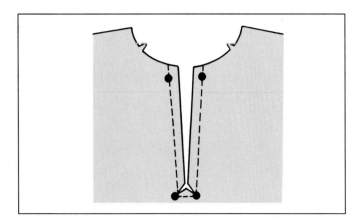

3. Interface the band sections, then press the seam allowance under on one long edge of the band section, trim to 5 mm (1/4").

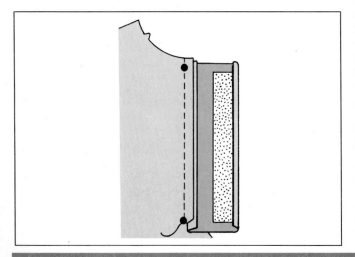

4. Pin the right side of the other long edge of the band to the wrong side of the garment, matching markings.

5. Machine stitch along the stitching line, ending exactly at the bottom marking. Trim and grade the seam allowances, then press them towards the band.

6. Fold the band to the outside of the garment and pin the pressed edge in place along the stitching line. Edge-stitch close to both long edges of the band, ending the stitching at the lower markings.

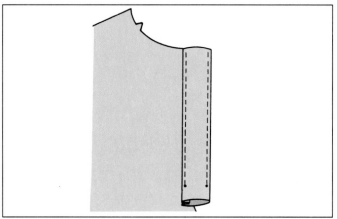

7. Attach the remaining band to the other side of the slashed opening in the same way.

8. Slip the ends of the bands to the inside of the garment. On the inside, lap the left band over the right. Pin the bands together above the lower markings.

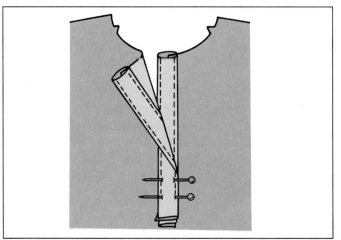

9. Working with the wrong side of garment face down, fold up the lower portion to expose the triangle at the bottom of the opening. Tack/baste the bands and the triangle together along the stitching line.

10. Machine stitch along the tacked/basted line, taking care not to catch the garment in the stitching. Press the seam flat, then downwards.

11. Turn to the right side and press. Make buttonholes on the right (top) band as required.

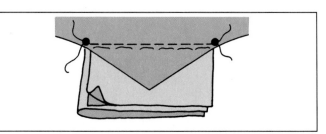

IX. Waistbands and Casings

Waistbands

There are several methods for applying and finishing waistbands. The method you use will depend upon the design of the garment and the fabric used.

To achieve a neat well-fitting waistband is difficult when there are many layers of fabric converging at the waistline seam. Each of the following methods solves this problem by eliminating the seam allowance on the waistband facing. The seam allowance for the following methods is 1.5 cm ($^5/_8$"). These methods are suitable for all fabrics, but are especially good for heavyweight or bulky fabrics.

Interfacing

Regardless of the method you use, the waistband must be interfaced so that it retains its shape. For best results, interface the entire waistband, eliminating the seam allowances as described under the chapter on Interfacings, (page 36).

If you are using a sew-in interfacing, add a row of tacking/basting stitches on the facing side of the waistband near the foldline. This will prevent the interfacing from moving.

Machine Stitched Method

1. Cut out the waistband and apply fusible or sew-in interfacing.
2. Trim off 5 mm ($^1/_4$") from the long unnotched edge, then finish the edge by over sewing, zig-zagging (see pages 27 and 33) or for a neater finish, using a seam binding (see page 34).

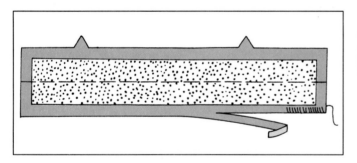

3. With right sides together, pin or tack/baste the notched waistband edge to the garment, matching notches, centres and markings; stitch.
4. Press the seam allowances towards the waistband, then trim the seam to 1 cm ($^3/_8$").

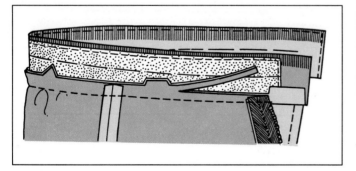

5. With right sides together, fold the waistband along the foldline and stitch the overlap end.
6. On the underlap turn the waistband seam allowance down. Beginning at the fold, stitch the end to 1 cm ($^3/_8$") from the lower edge. Pivot and continue stitching to the small dot marking. Back-stitch to secure. Clip the seam allowances to the dot marking and trim the seams.

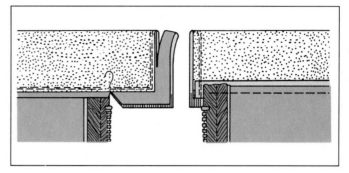

7. Turn the waistband right side out so that the finished edge extends 1 cm ($^3/_8$") below the waistband seam on the inside of the garment; press.
8. On the inside, fold the finished edge under diagonally at the opening. On the outside, pin the waistband layers together along the waistband seam.
9. On the outside, stitch in the groove (see page 26) of the waistband seam, catching the finished edge of the waistband and the diagonal turn-under, removing the pins as you stitch.

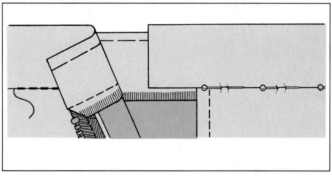

Hand Stitched Method

1. Cut out the waistband and apply fusible or sew-in interfacing.
2. Trim off 1.5 cm ($^5/_8$") from the long unnotched edge, then finish the edge by over sewing, zig-zagging (see pages 27 and 33) or for a neater finish, using a seam binding (see page 34).

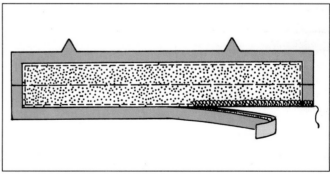

3. With right sides together, pin or tack/baste the notched waistband edge to the garment, matching notches, centres and markings; stitch.
4. Press the seam allowances towards the waistband. Trim the seam allowances to 1 cm ($^3/_8$").

IX. Waistbands and Casings

5. With right sides together, fold the waistband along the foldline. Stitch the ends (unfolding the seam allowance on the lapped end where it was pressed towards the waistband).

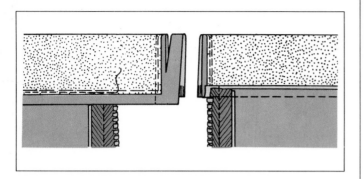

6. Turn the waistband right side out so that the finished edge meets the waistline seam on the inside of the garment. Pin and press.

7. On the inside, slip-stitch the finished edge in place along the entire length of the waistband seam, including the lap edge.

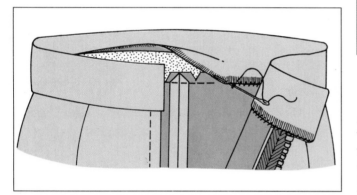

Casings and Elastic

When elastic or a draw-string is used to control fullness in a garment, it is often inserted in a tunnel of fabric called a casing. Elastic can, however be directly applied without a casing.

Casings

Casings can be formed from a separate strip of fabric sewn on, or made by folding an extension of the garment. The casing should be the same length as the garment area it is being attached to plus 5 mm (1/4") at each end seam allowance. It must be wide enough for the elastic or tape to pass through easily.

Folded Casings

These are usually found at waistline, sleeve, neck and trouser edges. The pattern will have an extra amount of material allowed to make the casing.

1. The raw edges are pressed under, then the edge is folded under again along the waistline or finished edge of the garment.

2. Edge-stitch along both folds to form the casing, leaving an opening along the lower edge to insert the elastic.

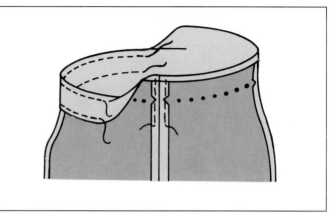

☆ TIP ☆

If your fabric is too bulky, scratchy or loosely woven for a folded casing, use the casing foldline as your seamline, and attach double folded bias tape, cutting off the excess fabric.

Applied Casings

These casings can be attached to the edge, middle, right or wrong side of the garment, depending on the design. The casing can also act as a facing when a strip is seamed to the edge of the garment. This technique is used in place of a folded casing if the garment edge is shaped or curved. The strip can be cut on the straight grain or the bias of the fabric, or could be a shaped facing. However the easiest method is to apply pre-packed bias tape.

To apply a casing to the edge of a garment

1. Fold in both ends of the casing.

2. With right sides together and starting at a seam pin the fold of the casing to the seamline of the garment. Stitch, then trim and grade the seam if necessary.

3. Fold the casing to the inside and pin in place.

4. Top-stitch close to both edges of the casing.

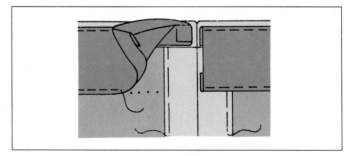

To apply a bias casing

Bias casings are often used on the inside of a one-piece dress, or the outside of a tunic or jacket to create a gathered waistline. A single fold bias tape or a strip of bias fabric is sewn to the garment a specified distance from the edge. If the bias casing is placed a short distance from the garment edge, a heading or ruffle, forms once the elastic is inserted.

1. Ensure the placement line for the casing is clearly marked.

2. Turn under the seam allowance at each end (and the edges if necessary) of the casing.

3. Starting at a seamline, pin the casing to the garment, along the placement line.

4. Edge-stitch along both sides of the casing.

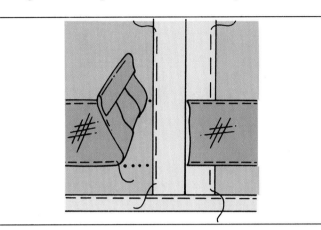

☆ **TIP** ☆

Before applying bias tape, use steam to pre-shape it into a curve that matches the garment edge, (see Bindings on page 46).

Inserting the elastic or tape

Select elastic that is approximately 5 mm (1/4") narrower than your casing. Cut the elastic 2.5 cm (1") longer than the body measurement.

1. Fasten a safety pin to one end of the elastic and push-pull it through the casing.

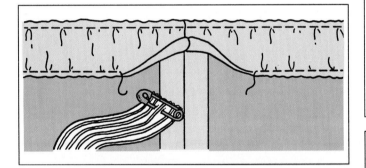

2. To avoid accidently pulling the elastic right through, pin the other end to the garment just below the opening in the casing.

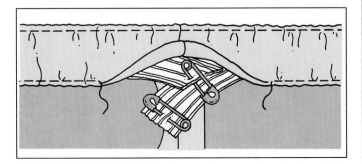

3. Overlap the ends of the elastic and stitch them together securely.

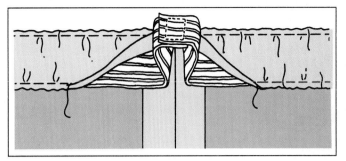

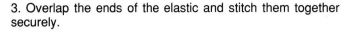

Closing the casing

Once the elastic has been inserted close the opening.

For a folded casing stretch the elastic slightly, and carefully edge stitch across the opening, taking care not to catch the elastic in the stitching.

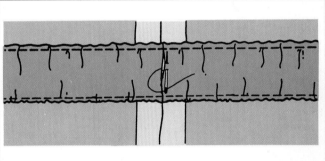

For an applied casing, slip-stitch the ends of the casing together, taking care not to catch the elastic.

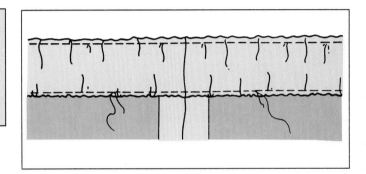

☆ **TIP** ☆

To prevent the elastic rolling inside the casing during wear, position the fullness evenly then stitch in the seam grooves through the elastic.

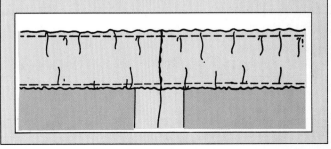

X. Belts and Carriers

Direct Application of Elastic

With this method you stitch right through the elastic on to the garment stretching the elastic as you sew.

It is a quick technique particularly suitable for waistbands and cuffs of lingerie or knitted sports wear, which have extended facings.

1. Cut the elastic to the required length, generally about 8 cm (3") smaller than the actual body measurement. This allows for an overlap. Overlap the ends by 1.5 cm (1/2") and stitch securely together.

2. Trim the garment seam allowance to match the width of the elastic.

3. Divide the elastic and garment edge into four to eight sections and mark.

4. Pin the elastic to the wrong side of the garment, matching marks, and with the elastic edge level with the fabric edge.

5. Use a zig-zag, stretch stitch or straight stitch to stitch the elastic to the garment, stretching the elastic to fit as you sew.

6. Fold the elastic to the inside of the garment and stitch it in place close to the raw edges. Again, stretch the elastic to fit as you sew.

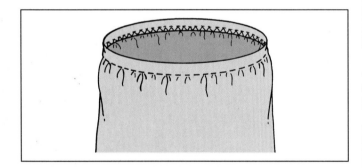

Belts

Belts can be an attractive addition to many garments. A combination of garment design and personal preference will determine the type of belt you choose.

Tie Belts

These are the easiest to make and the width and length are personal choices.

1. Cut the fabric twice the chosen width, and long enough to tie, plus seam allowances.

2. With right sides together, fold in half lengthwise.

3. Stitch ends and along the seamline, leaving an opening at the centre for turning through. Secure the stitches at either side of the opening by back-stitching.

4. Trim seams and corners and press.

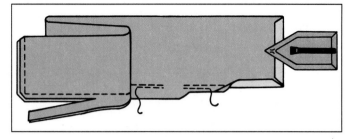

5. Pull to the right side through the opening and press. Slip-stitch the opening closed.

Interfaced Belts

For this type of belt, some sort of fastening is required. Haberdashery departments sell a wide range of belt buckles and fastenings. It is advisable to choose the buckle before making the belt, because the widths of buckles may vary. Interfaced belts can be either straight or shaped.

1. Cut two strips of fabric on the lengthwise grain. The length should be the waist measurement plus about 20 cm (8") and the width as required, both plus seam allowances.

2. Cut two strips of heavyweight interfacing, the finished width and length without any seam allowance.

3. Stitch the strips of interfacing together with rows of stitches 5 mm (1/4") apart.

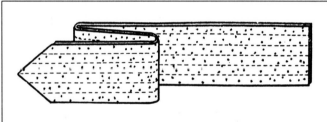

4. Pin the interfacing in the centre of the wrong side of belt section. Fold the belt seam allowances over interfacing, notch point if necessary. Tack/baste along the seamline.

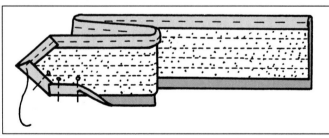

5. Stay-stitch the belt facing along the seamline. Fold the seam allowances plus an extra 2 mm (1/8") to the wrong side and press. Trim and notch the seam allowances.

6. Centre the belt facing over the belt and pin in place.

7. Edge-stitch, or top-stitch close to the finished edge.

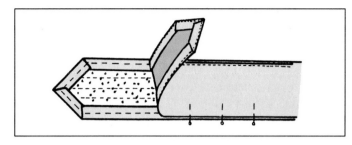

It is possible to substitute a strip of belting for the interfacing and these are available in many different weights and widths.

Buckles

There are many types of fastenings for belts; buckles with or without prongs, clasp buckles, hooks and eyes and snap fasteners.

Fitting a prong buckle

1. Pierce a hole through the centre of the belt 5 cm (2") from the end to which the buckle will be attached.

2. Work buttonhole stitch (see page 80) around the hole to neaten it.

3. Slip the buckle prong through the hole, fold back the end and secure with two rows of stitching.

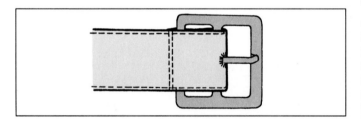

4. On the tab end of the belt make an eyelet at the centre front, and then one or two either side of this about 5 cm (2") away. For a professional finish use commercially bought eyelets, alternatively hand finish eyelets as given above.

Clasp Buckle

1. Slip the ends of the belt through both halves of the buckle.

2. Fold the ends of the belt over the bars, try on and adjust the fit if required.

3. Trim the ends to 2.5 cm (1"), and then stitch them in place securely, whip stitch over raw edges to finish and keep in place.

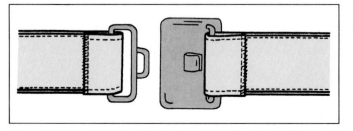

Belt Carriers

Belt loops will help a belt stay in place when it is worn. If you are adding a belt to a garment, the loops should be centred over the waistline, or required position. Plan on three or four loops on the waistband of a skirt or trousers, and one at each side seam for a dress. If the buckle is heavy you might need to add extra carriers midway between the side seams and the centre front.

Fabric carriers can be used as a design feature, whereas carriers that are worked in thread matching the belt, are less visible.

Mark the position of the carriers on the garment.

Fabric carriers

1. Cut a strip of fabric from the lengthwise grain, twice the required width plus 1 cm ($1/2$") seam allowance. The length should be the width of the belt, plus 2.5 cm (1"), multiplied by the number of carriers needed.

2. Fold the fabric in half lengthwise, with right sides together and stitch 5 mm ($1/4$") from the edge. Trim seam allowances to 3 mm ($1/8$").

3. Turn through to the right side and centring the seam, press. If required edge-stitch along both folded edges. Cut into the required number of carriers.

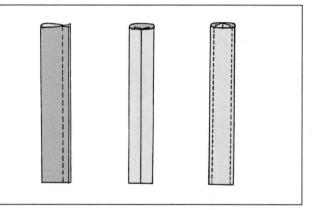

4. With right side up place the cut end of the carrier 3 mm ($1/8$") below the top edge of the waistband at required position. Back stitching at each side, stitch 3 mm ($1/8$") from cut end, taking care not to stitch beyond the edges. Trim close to the stitching.

5. Fold the carrier upwards along the stitching line. Using a small closely spaced zig-zag, stitch close to the fold enclosing the raw edge.

6. Fold carrier down and attach the other end in the same way.

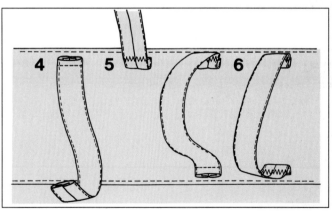

Thread Carriers

There are two methods of making thread carriers, see Thread Loops on page 84. The loops should be attached to the seam of the garment.

XI. Sleeves and Cuffs

Sleeves

There are three main sleeve types - differentiated by the way they are joined to the garment. Kimono sleeves are cut as part of the front and back of the garment. Raglan sleeves are joined to the body pieces by a shaped diagonal seam. Set in sleeves fit in to the armhole of the front and back of the garment. The shape at the top edge, or sleeve head depends on the design of the garment, but is shaped to fall smoothly over the shoulder.

If your sleeve has an opening for a cuff, this is usually made before the sleeve seam is sewn, (see page 64). The cuff is then attached after the seam has been completed.

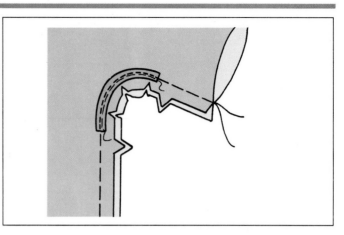

Kimono Sleeves

1. With right sides together pin the garment front to the back at the shoulders. Stitch seams, press and finish the raw edges.

2. Pin the side/underarm seams, matching raw edges, notches and markings

3. Reinforce the underarm area with small stitches or by tacking/basting a piece of tape or seam binding over the centre 10 to 15 cm (4" to 6") of the curved area.

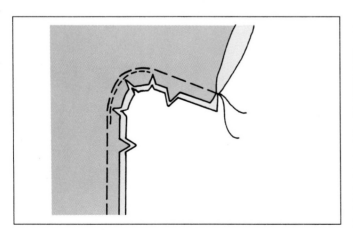

4. Beginning at the lower edge of the garment, stitch the underarm/side seam, shortening the stitch slightly along the length of the tape.

5. Clip the curves and press the seam open. Do **not** clip the seam binding.

Raglan Sleeves

Some raglan sleeves have a dart at the top to give a smoother fit over the shoulder. This can also be achieved by having a seam that runs from the neckline to the lower edge, over the shoulder.

1. Stitch the shoulder dart or seam and the underarm seam, press and finish the edges.

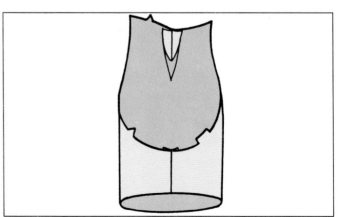

2. Turn the sleeve right side out and the garment inside out. Slip the sleeve inside the armhole and pin together, matching underarm seams and notches.

3. Stitch the seam, then reinforce the seam between the notches with a second row of stitches, 3 mm (1/8") inside the seam allowance.

4. Clip the seam allowance at notches and trim between these clips, close to the second line of stitching.

5. Finish the raw edges then press the seam allowances open above the notches.

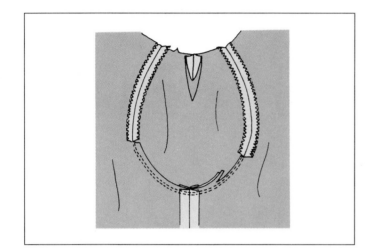

Set-in Sleeves

Most set-in sleeves have an amount of excess fabric at the sleeve head that requires either easing in, gathering or tucking according to the design.

This extra fabric occurs between the notches marked on the pattern. In an untailored, loose fitting blouse the amount of ease may be very slight and consequently the sleeve head curve very shallow. On a more tailored jacket or shirt the sleeve head may be higher. In either case it is important to ease the fullness in evenly.

Easing the fullness

It is much easier to ease the sleeve head if you do it before stitching the underarm seam.

1. Working on the right side of the fabric, ease-stitch the sleeve head first along the seamline between the notches, then 5 mm (1/4") away, within the seam allowance. Be sure to leave the threads long enough to pull up to create the sleeve head.

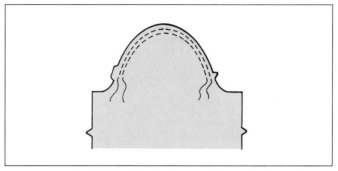

2. Stitch the sleeve seam and press open the finished seams.

3. Finish the lower edge of the sleeve according to the design.

Inserting the sleeve

1. Turn the sleeve right side out and turn the garment inside out.

2. Slip the sleeve inside the armhole and pin them together at the sleeve and garment underarm seams, the shoulder markings and notches.

3. Draw up the ease-stitching by pulling the threads at each end, sliding the fabric along to distribute the fullness evenly to fit the armhole.

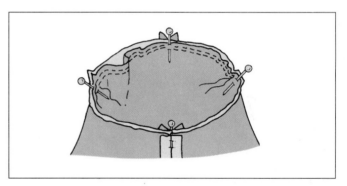

4. Pin closely all around the sleeve hole. Hand tack/baste along the seamline, remove the pins and check the fit.

Stitching the sleeve

1. With the sleeve side up, begin at the underarm seam and stitch along the seamline. As you stitch, use your fingers on either side of the presser foot to keep the eased area from puckering under the needle.

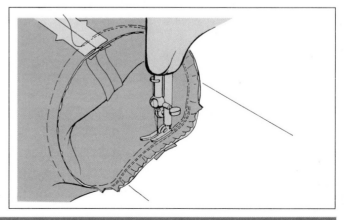

XI. Sleeves and Cuffs

2. When you reach the underarm seam, overlap the stitches.

3. Stitch a second row 3 mm (1/8") away from the first, within the seam allowance.

4. Trim the seam allowance close to the stitching in the underarm area between the notches.

5. To strengthen and reinforce the underarm area, it is wise to finish the seam allowances between the notches with a row of machine zig-zag stitch or overcast the edges. If your fabric frays finish the entire armhole this way.

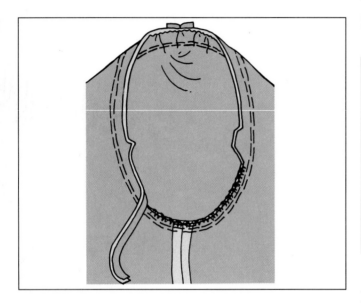

Pressing the sleeve

1. With the sleeve side up, place the upper portion of the armhole seam (the sleeve head) over the end of a sleeve board, or ironing board.

2. With the point of the iron press over the seam allowances. Use steam, if appropriate for your fabric, or a damp cloth, to blend the stitching and shrink out some of the fullness. The seam allowances should turn towards the sleeve.

☆ TIPS ☆

The shallower the curve of the sleeve head the less ease the sleeve has. If your sleeve has very little ease, you may find it easier to attach it to the garment **before** the underarm and side seams are stitched. Once the sleeve is attached the garment side seam and underarm sleeve seam are stitched in one continuous operation.

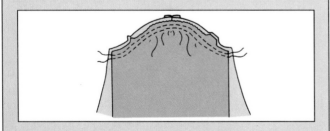

If you are working with a stretch fabric, forget about ease-stitching. Working with the garment side up, pin the sleeve to the armhole edge, matching markings. As you stitch, ease in the fullness by stretching the armhole to fit the sleeve head.

Sleeve Openings for Cuffs

Sleeve edges can be finished in many different ways. If a snug fitting cuff is required an opening is needed at the lower edge of the sleeve. The edge of this opening can be finished in a number of ways.

Seam Opening

The simplest type of opening is one made in the sleeve seam. The seam is stitched to a point about 4 to 8 cm (1½" to 3") above the cuff edge, then the entire seam is pressed open. The seam does not overlap.

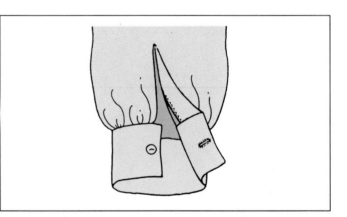

Faced Placket

On this type of placket opening the edges meet rather than overlap.

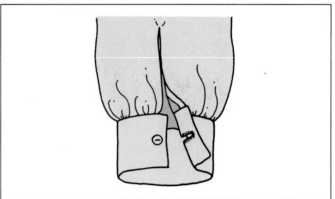

1. Cut a piece of garment fabric 6.5 cm (2½") wide by the length of the sleeve opening plus 2.5 cm (1"). Finish the raw edges (see pages 33 and 34) along the sides and top edge. With right sides together, place the facing over the slash markings on the sleeve.

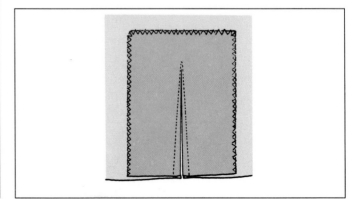

2. Stitch along the stitching lines taking one stitch across the point. Slash to the point (without cutting the stitching) and turn the facing right side out; press.

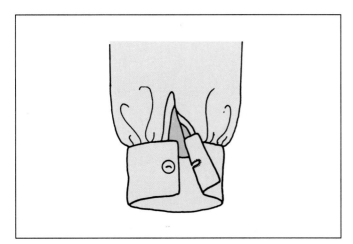

Continuous Bound Placket

A narrow strip of fabric is attached to the sleeve edge to give a narrow lap.

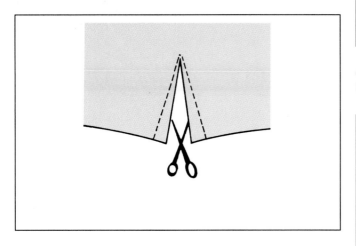

1. Cut a strip of fabric for the binding approximately 4 cm (1 1/2") wide and twice the length of the opening.

2. Stitch along the stitching lines either side of the slash using small reinforcement stitches and taking one stitch across the point. Slash to the point (without cutting the stitching).

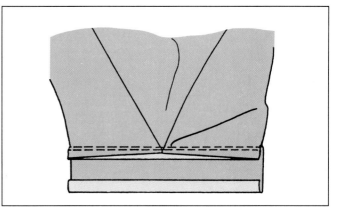

3. Spread the edges of the opening so they almost form a straight line. With right sides together, pin the facing strip to the opening edge, then stitch, using small stitches approximately 5 mm (1/4") from the raw edges.

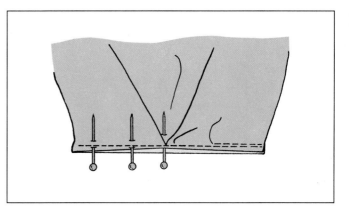

4. Grade the seam, and press the seam allowances towards the binding strip.

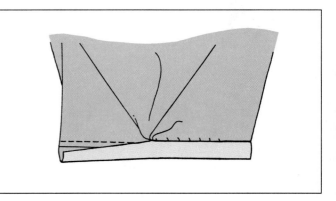

5. Press under 5 mm (1/4") on remaining raw edge of strip, pin over the seam on the inside of the sleeve. Slip-stitch in place.

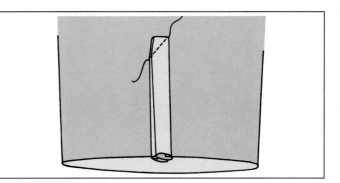

6. Stitch diagonally across the top of the fold to prevent the binding strip from turning to the outside.

7. Press the front portion of the lap to the inside and tack/baste in place across the lower edge of the sleeve.

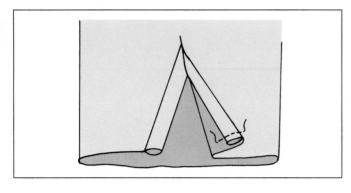

Hemmed Opening

Some patterns have a sleeve opening that is formed by hemming part of the seam allowance so that when the cuff is buttoned a small tuck is formed on the sleeve.

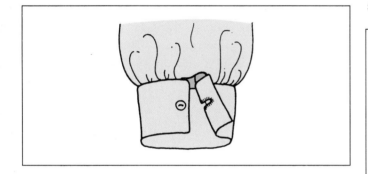

1. Reinforce along the seamline extending 1.5 cm (5/8") beyond the markings for the opening.

2. Clip to the stitching at the markings.

3. Turn under the raw edges between the clips and fold again along stitching line to form a narrow hem. Slip-stitch in place; press.

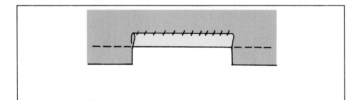

Tailored Placket

This method is used on shirt sleeves and neck openings. It can look very professional if worked with precision and care.

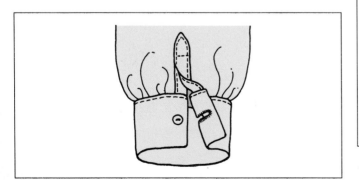

1. With small stitches reinforce the sleeve opening along the seamlines. Slash to within 1 cm (1/2") of the stitching at the top, then carefully clip into the corners.

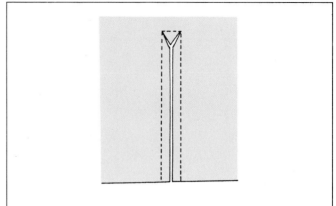

2. Place right side of the underlap piece to the wrong side of the back edge of the sleeve. Stitch, then trim and press the seam allowances towards the underlap.

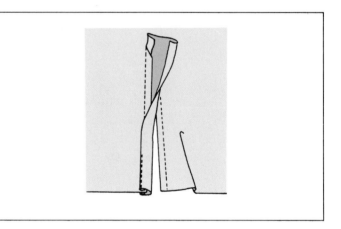

3. Turn under the seam allowance of the long edge and press. Fold the pressed edge to the right side, over the seam allowances and edge-stitch through all thicknesses.

4. Place the right side of the overlap piece to the wrong side of the remaining slashed edge. Stitch, then trim and press the seam towards the overlap.

5. Stitch the end of the overlap to the base of the triangular end of the slash. Press the stitched end of the overlap up.

6. Turn in the seam allowances of the overlap, press and tack/baste. Fold the overlap to the stitching line and pin.

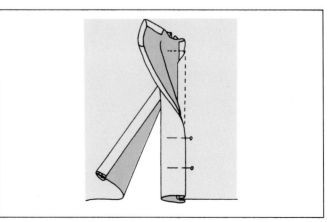

7. Stitch the outside fold of the underlap to the top of the

opening, making sure the underlap is not caught in stitching.

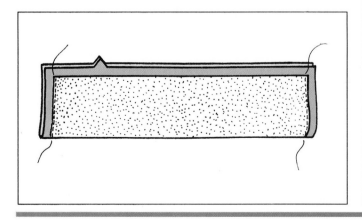

8. Pull threads to the wrong side and tie securely. Working through all the thicknesses, stitch across the placket, securing both the top of the underlap and the point of the slash in the stitches; turn and following the direction of the arrows on the diagram stitch along the remaining edges of the overlap. Pull the ends to the wrong side and tie securely.

Cuffs

Cuffs can be loose fitting without an opening or snug fitting with an opening that requires fastening. Either way they are faced and often also interfaced. A cuff with an opening often has the lower edge of the sleeve gathered or pleated into it. The facing of a loose fitting cuff is often made by extending the material of the lower edge of the sleeve.

If bound buttonholes (see page 77) are required these should be worked before the cuff is made.

Cuffs with Plackets

Using your cuff pattern piece as a guide, cut your interfacing, (without seam allowance for fusible interfacing), see Interfacings on page 36.

1. Press the seam allowance of the notched edge of the facing to the inside.

Note: To use the machine finished shirt sleeve method press the seam allowance of the notched edge of the **cuff** to the inside.

For a one piece cuff

2. Fold the cuff lengthwise, along the foldline, and with right sides together pin or tack/baste the side edges; stitch.

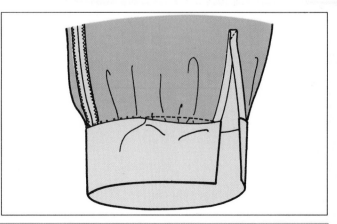

For a two piece cuff

2. With right sides together, pin or tack/baste around the edge of the cuff, leaving the notched edge open; stitch.

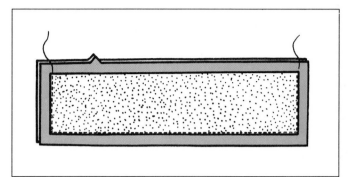

For both cuffs

3. Trim and grade the seam allowances, press open and then towards the facing.
4. Turn the cuffs through to the right side and press.

Attaching the Cuff

Having sewn the sleeve underarm seam, finished the edges and gathered or pleated the cuff edge, you are ready to attach the cuff. There are two basic methods of doing this, the first involves hand finishing, the second is machine finished.

Hand Finished Method

1. With right sides together, pin the cuff to the sleeve, matching notches and distributing gathers evenly.

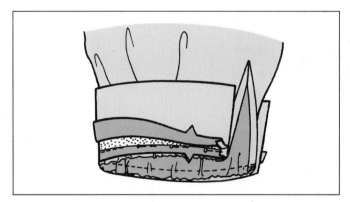

2. Stitch, then trim and grade the seam allowances. Press the allowances towards the cuff.

3. Then working on the inside, slip-stitch the facing in place over the seam allowances.

XI. Sleeves and Cuffs

Machine Finished Method

This method of attaching a cuff is used on shirt sleeves.

1. Pin the cuff facing to the wrong side of the lower sleeve edge, matching notches and distributing gathers evenly.

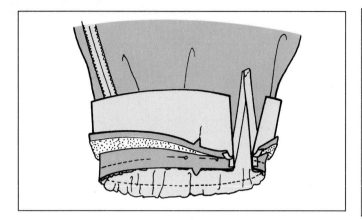

2. Stitch, then trim and grade the seam allowances. Press the allowances towards the cuff.

3. Then working on the outside, fold the cuff over the seam allowances to the stitching line, pin. Then edge-stitch the cuff in place.

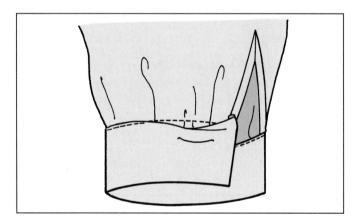

Cuffs without Plackets

Cuffs without plackets have no opening and therefore have to be large enough for the hand or arm to slip in and out.

1. Interface the cuff section, then with right sides together stitch the ends of the cuff together.

2. Fold up the notched edge of the facing.

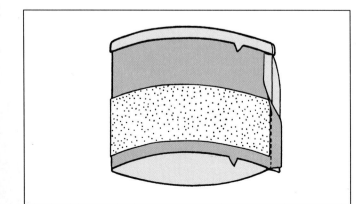

3. Gather or tuck the cuff edge of the sleeve section as required. Stitch the underarm seam, press open and finish.

4. Then with right sides together pin the cuff to the sleeve edge matching seams and notches; stitch.

5. Trim and grade seam allowances, press towards the cuff.

6. Then working on the inside, slip-stitch the facing in place over the seam allowances.

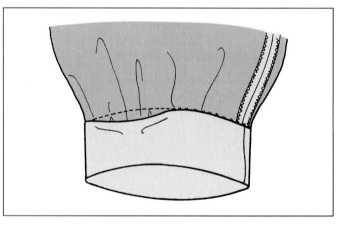

Mock Turned Up Cuffs

If your pattern has straight untapered sleeves (or legs), and you want to have turn-ups, this is an easy way to fake them with the minimum of additional fabric required.

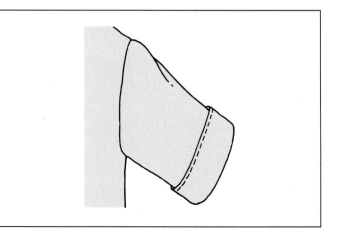

1. Before cutting out your garment you will need to alter the

pattern. Cut along the hemline and spread it 1.5 cm (1/2") apart and insert a strip of paper.

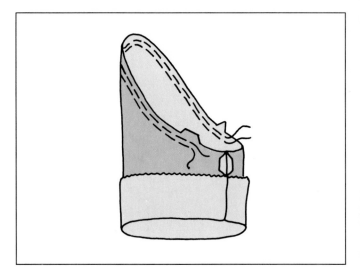

2. When you come to hem your garment, fold the edge to the inside along the hemline and press.

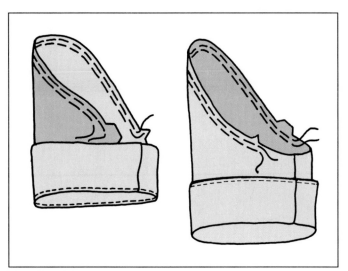

3. Fold the edge up again by the same amount and press.
4. Stitch 5 to 6mm (1/4") from the second fold. This will create a tuck and encase the raw edge of the hem.

5. Open out the sleeve to press the tuck up and the cuff down.

Pockets

Pockets should be more than just an attractive design feature. In order to be functional they should be constructed so that they can withstand the wear and tear of frequent use.

Patch Pockets

Patch pockets can be made in an assortment of shapes and sizes, creating design interest on skirts, blouses, jackets and trousers. They can be lined, unlined or self-lined. Patch pockets can be made in many ways depending on the design and fabric choice.

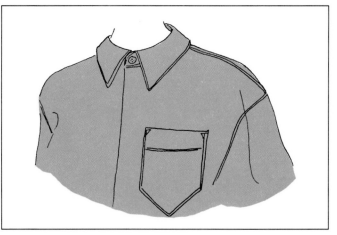

Unlined Patch Pockets

Unlined pockets are the easiest to make. They are particularly popular on casual clothes and children's garments in light to mediumweight fabrics.
1. Press under 5 mm (1/4") on the upper edge of the pocket and edge-stitch.

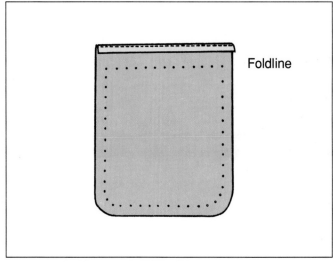

Foldline

2. Fold the upper edge to the right side along the foldline; press.
3. Starting at the fold, stitch along the seamline, back-stitching at the beginning and end.
4. Trim the seam allowances in the facing area only to 5 mm (1/4"). If your fabric is bulky, diagonally trim the corners.
The shape of the pocket determines the way it is finished.

XII. Pockets

Curved Patch Pockets

5. Make a row of machine gathering stitches around the curved edges within the seam allowance and approximately 5 mm (1/4") from the seamline stitches.

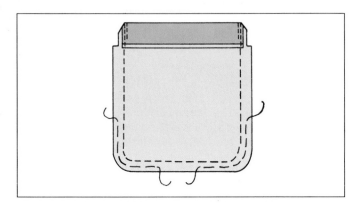

6. Turn the facing to the wrong side, pushing the upper corners out. (A knitting needle will help).

7. Pull up the gathering threads to shape the curve, then press under along the seamline, rolling the stitching to the wrong side. Press the facing seams and the fold.

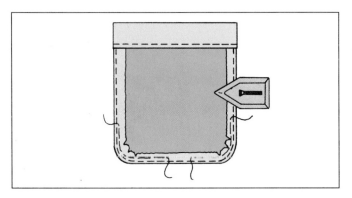

8. To eliminate bulk, notch out the fullness in the seam allowance at the curves as far as the machine tacking/basting stitches.

9. Edge-stitch or top-stitch the facing in place, or secure it to the pocket with a strip of fusible web.

☆ TIP ☆

To help the finished pocket retain its shape and provide you with an accurate guide for shaping the curves or mitring the corners, cut a lightweight fusible interfacing from the pocket pattern piece, without any seam allowance and omitting the facing. Fuse this to the pocket.

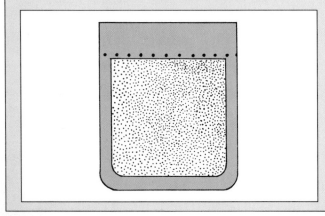

Square or Rectangular Patch Pockets

5. Mitre the lower corners, as described on page 50.

6. Edge-stitch or top-stitch the facing in place, or secure it to the pocket with a strip of fusible web.

Lined Pockets

There are times when a pocket lining makes a nice finish. You can add this touch even if your pattern does not include it.

1. Once the pocket is cut out, fold the pocket pattern piece along the foldline to omit the facing. Use this new shape to cut the lining.

2. Fold the upper edge of the lining under. The width of this fold should be equal to half the depth of the original pocket facing; press.

3. With right sides together, pin the lining to the pocket, matching sides and lower edge. Turn the pocket facing down over the lining so that all the raw edges match, pin.

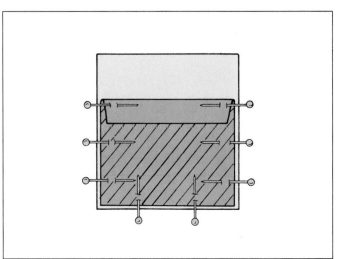

4. Starting at the fold, stitch along the seamline, back-stitching at the ends.

5. Trim the seam allowances and corners, notch any curves.

6. Press the lining seam allowance towards the lining.

7. Turn the pocket right side out and press, rolling the seam slightly to the lining side.

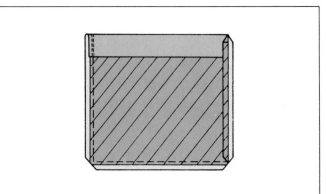

8. Slip-stitch the lining to the facing at the opening.

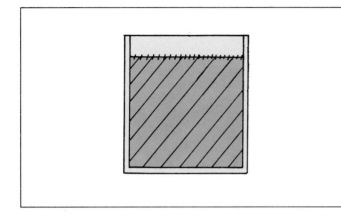

Stitch both sides and the bottom edge leaving a small opening.

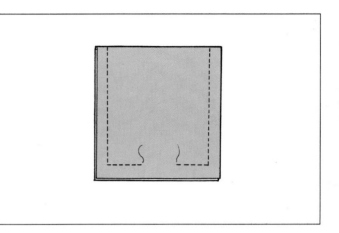

3. Trim, clip and notch as for the lined pocket, then turn the pocket to the right side through the opening.

4. Slip-stitch the opening closed. Press, rolling the seam towards the side you wish to use as the pocket lining.

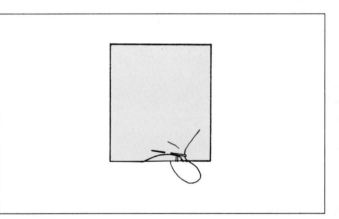

☆ **TIP** ☆

Trim 3 mm (¹/₈") off the sides and lower edge of the pocket lining. Pin the lining to the pocket, matching the raw edges, and proceed as described above. The smaller lining will automatically cause the seams to roll slightly to the inside.

Self-lined Pockets

This easy way to line a pocket works best on lightweight fabrics. If your pattern does not utilise this technique you can easily convert it.

1. When you cut out a pocket, place the pattern piece so that the foldline is on a crosswise fold of the fabric so that the facing extends beyond the fold and will not be cut.

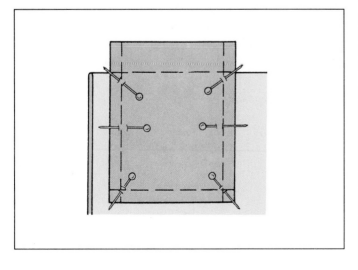

2. To make the pocket, fold it in half with right sides together.

Attaching Patch Pockets

The easiest way to attach the pocket is to top-stitch or edge-stitch it to the garment.

1. Pin or tack/baste the pocket in place.

2. Edge-stitch and/or top-stitch 2 mm to 1 cm (¹/₈" to ³/₈") from the edge.

3. To reinforce the upper corners, back-stitch or machine stitch a small triangle.

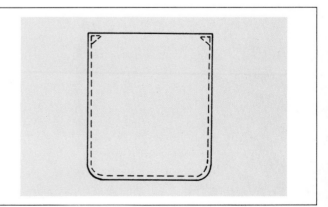

XII. Pockets

On delicate or difficult to handle fabrics, such as corduroy, it is easier to apply the pocket by hand. To do this, pin or hand tack/baste the pocket in place. Turn back the pocket edge slightly and slip-stitch it to the garment. To secure, take several small stitches at the upper corners of the pocket.

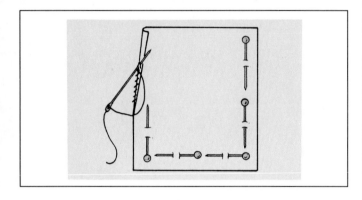

In-seam Pockets

In-seam pockets are found at the side seams of dresses, skirts and trousers. Usually these pockets are created from a separate pattern piece that can be cut from a lining fabric, which is then stitched to an extension to the pocket opening, or to the seamline.

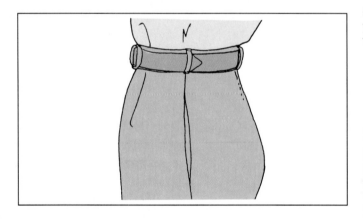

1. Reinforce the wrong side of the front of the garment section along the seamline with tape.
2. With right sides together and matching markings, pin then stitch the pocket pieces to the front and back garment sections.

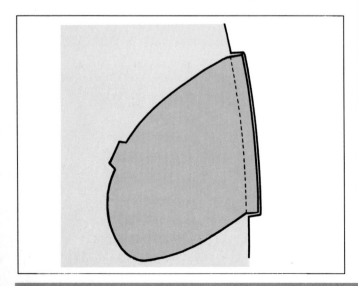

3. Press seams open. Then with right sides together, pin the garment sections and the pocket pieces, matching notches and markings.
4. Stitch the side seams above and below the pocket, reinforcing the seam at the pocket marking by back-stitching.
5. Starting from the lower edge, stitch round the pocket extension, reinforcing the corners by shortening your stitch length for about 2.5 cm (1") on either side of each corner.

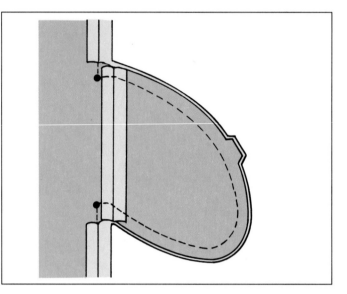

Clip the garment/pocket back seam allowance **only** so that you can press the side seams open and the pocket towards the front of the garment.

Cut-in-one Pockets

Some patterns have the pocket shape built into the front and back pattern pieces. This saves time because you do not have to cut out the pockets separately or stitch them to the garment. You can adjust separate in-seam pockets to this method as long as your fabric is wide enough.

1. Lap the pocket pattern piece over the garment front pattern piece, matching the seamlines and markings. Pin or tape together. Repeat for the garment back.

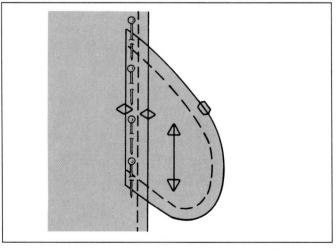

2. Cut out the front and back garment sections.

3. Reinforce the garment front with tape or interfacing to prevent the fabric stretching.

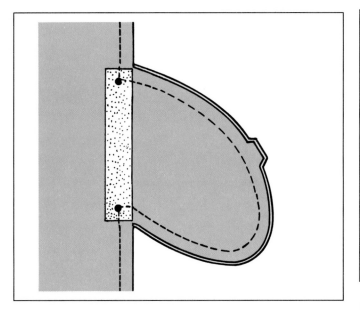

4. Sew the garment together following the guidelines for In-seam Pockets.

Front Hip Pockets

Many skirts and trousers feature hip-line pockets, sometimes called slant pockets. The slanted opening may be straight or curved.

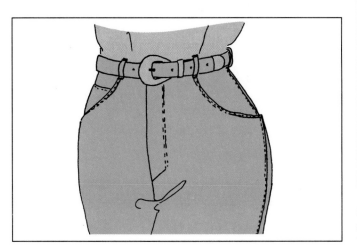

Front hip pockets consist of two differently shaped pieces - the pocket, which also becomes part of the main section of the garment at the waistline, and the pocket facing, which finishes the opening edge.

If your garment fabric is heavy or bulky, cut the pocket facing from lightweight lining fabric in a matching colour.

1. Stay-stitch the pocket edge. For very stretchy or very delicate fabric or if the pocket is going to get a lot of use reinforce the pocket edge. Cut a strip of interfacing 5 cm (2") wide and shaped to follow the opening edge of the pocket. Tack/baste or fuse it along the opening edge of the pocket.

2. With right sides together matching markings, stitch the pocket facing to the garment front.

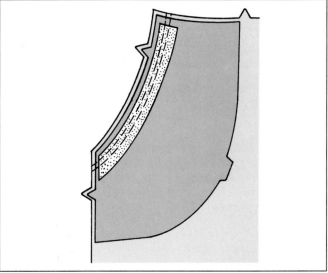

3. Trim and grade the seam allowances. Clip and notch curves if required.

4. Press the seam open, then press the seam allowances towards the facing.

5. Under-stitch the facing to the seam allowances.

6. Fold the facing to the inside, if required top-stitch along the finished edge.

7. With right sides together, pin the pocket to the facing; stitch. Press and then finish the raw edges.

8. Pin then tack/baste the pocket to the garment at top and side edges.

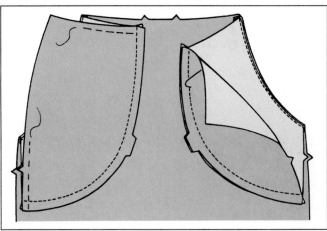

9. Pin the front and back garment pieces together. Stitch ensuring the pocket and facing are caught in the seam.

The upper edge of the pocket should be treated as part of the garment when stitching the waistline seam.

Single Welt Pocket

This type of pocket has a single strip of fabric that is pressed up over the pocket opening. The pocket is cut in one piece, double the depth of the pocket plus 2.5 cm (1"), and 2.5 cm (1") wider than the opening.

XII. Pockets

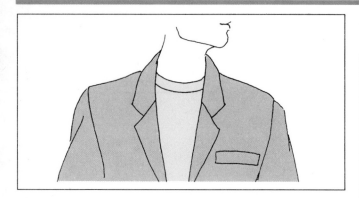

It is very important to make precise markings, and stitch accurately, carefully cutting and pressing at each stage.

For a crisp finish interface the outer half of the welt piece. It may also be helpful to centre a piece of interfacing, over the pocket markings, to the wrong side of the garment, approximately 5 cm (2") larger than the opening.

1. Fold the welt in half with right sides together and stitch the ends. Trim the seam allowances, then turn and press.

2. On the right side of the garment place the seamline of the welt over the lower stitching line, pin then tack/baste.

3. With right sides together, pin then tack/baste the pocket over the welt, with the deeper section above the welt.

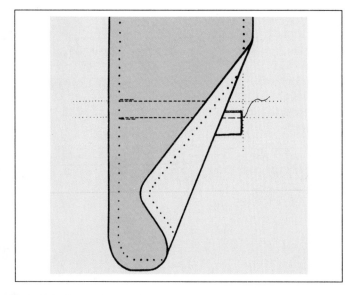

4. Stitch the pocket to the garment, through the welt along the lower stitching line, back-stitching at each end, then sew the other stitching line in the same way.

5. Slash through the centre, to within 1 cm (1/2") of the ends, and clip diagonally into the corners.

6. Turn the pocket to the inside, and pull on the triangular ends to square the corners. Turn the welt up and press.

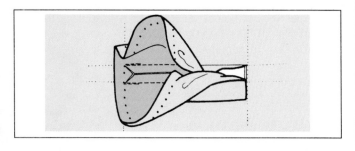

7. Matching pocket edges, pin together, then stitch, taking care to catch the base of the triangles in the stitching. Trim and finish the raw edges.

8. On the right side slip-stitch the ends of the welt in place.

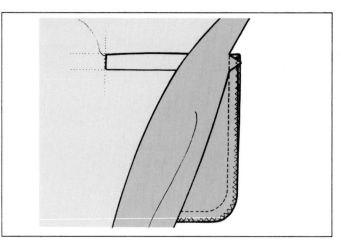

Bound Pockets

This type of pocket looks like a large bound buttonhole from the right side, with two narrow strips of fabric meeting in the centre of the opening. Lining fabric can be used for the lower pocket piece to reduce bulk.

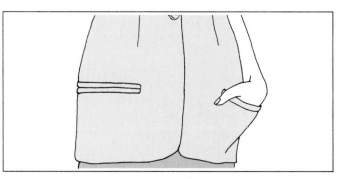

It is very important to make precise markings, and stitch accurately, carefully cutting and pressing at each stage.

1. Cut two pocket sections, one in lining fabric, the required pocket depth and width, plus 1 cm (1/2") all round for seam allowance, the second in garment fabric to have an extra 5 to 6 cm (2" to 2 1/2") added to the depth, plus 1 cm (1/2") all round for seam allowance.

2. With right sides together pin the longest pocket piece upside down over the pocket markings with the straight edge extending 2.5 cm (1") below the lower stitching line.

3. On the right side of the garment, stitch around the marked opening, starting at the centre, and pivoting at the corners.

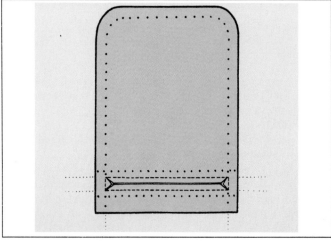

Slash through the centre to within 1 cm (1/2") of each end, then carefully clip diagonally to the corners, taking care not to cut the stitches.

4. Turn the pocket to the inside and pull on the small triangular ends to square the corners. Press the seam allowances and triangles away from the opening.

5. Fold the pocket and straight edge towards the centre and make two equal sized pleats. Check on the right side that the pleats or lips are even then tack/baste in place. Whip stitch the edges together.

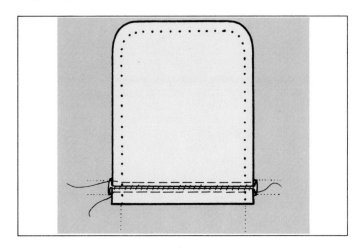

6. On the right side fold the garment back and stitch the triangles to the ends of the pleats along the stitching line, then stitch the top seam allowances to the pocket close to the original stitching line.

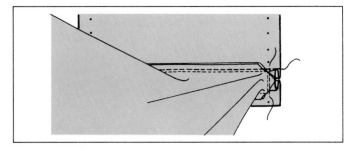

7. Pin the pocket lining section to the straight edge of the attached piece, then stitch through the seam allowances, and both pocket pieces close to the original stitching line.

8. Turn down the pocket lining and press, then turn down the pocket piece and match edges. Pin, then stitch together, catching the triangular ends in the seam. Finish the raw edges.

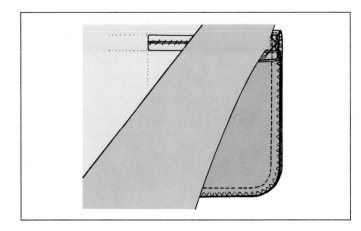

9. Turn to the right side and press. Remove all tacking/basting stitches.

Fastenings

How you choose to fasten your garment can play an important role in the finished appearance. Fastenings can be simply functional and discreet or a deliberate design statement. You can choose ornamental or contrasting buttons, or go for matching or self covered buttons. A visit to a well stocked notions or haberdashery department may inspire your decision. The options could include toggles, frogs, bow ties, snap fasteners, velcro, hooks and eyes, buttons or zips. Of course your pattern and garment fabric will dictate to a certain extent but ultimately the choice is yours.

Buttons and Buttonholes

The type of buttonhole you use will depend on the design and the fabric type of the garment and your sewing ability. Generally machine worked buttonholes are suitable for most garments, bound buttonholes are used for tailored garments and and hand worked buttonholes are used for fine fabrics.

1. Stick to the size of button recommended for the pattern. The buttonhole should measure the diameter plus the thickness of the button plus about 3 mm (1/8"). Therefore, a domed 1.5 cm (5/8") button will require a slightly larger buttonhole than a flat button of the same size.

2. Always make a test buttonhole on a scrap of garment fabric first using the same number of layers, including any interfacing or lining.

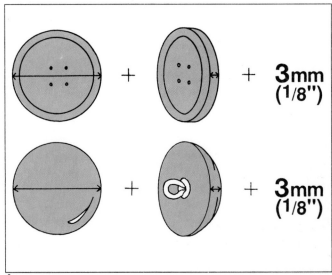

3. Always mark the buttonhole positions on to the right side of the fabric. Check the markings are accurate and equally spaced.

On women's garments buttonholes are on the right hand side, on men's the buttonholes are on the left.

Positioning Buttonholes

Buttons and buttonholes are usually placed in relation to the garment centre line. Therefore when a garment is fastened the centre lines must meet. Buttonholes should be placed near the top (neck edge), near the bottom of the garment, (but not through the hem thickness) and at stress points, like the fullest part of the bust or at the waist. Any other buttons should be spaced evenly between (at least 1.5 cm (5/8") apart).

XIII. Fastenings

Horizontal buttonholes extend 3 mm ($1/8$") from the centre line towards the garment edge, to allow for the garment to 'pull' away from the closing. The buttons are placed on the centre line.

Vertical buttonholes are placed on the centre line with the button 3 mm ($1/8$") below the top of the buttonhole.

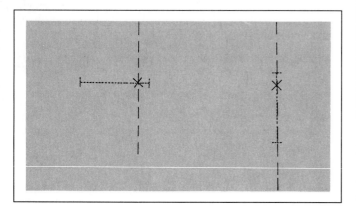

☆ TIP ☆

Check the markings that you made at the cutting out stage by placing the pattern tissue on the garment. Stick pins straight through the tissue at both ends of the buttonhole then remove the pattern without removing the pins.

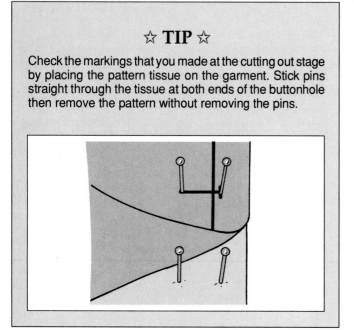

Machine Buttonholes

Machine buttonholes are worked once the facings are in place and through all layers of fabric. The following steps are basic guidelines for machine made buttonholes, but check your machine manual.

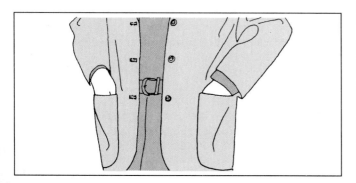

1. Position the needle to the left of centre and use a close

zig-zag stitch set at half width to stitch along one side of the buttonhole.

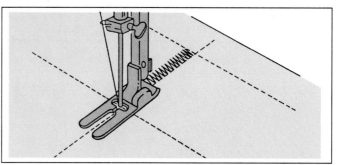

2. At the end of this side, lower the needle into the fabric on the right side. Lift the presser foot and pivot the fabric around. Lower the presser foot, lift the needle, make a few stitches at full width to form an end bar, ending with the needle at the outer edge of the buttonhole.

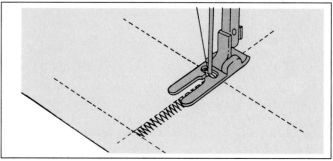

3. Lift the needle, re-set the stitch width to half and stitch the other side of the buttonhole. Finish with full width stitches to form an end bar, as before.

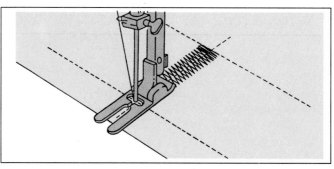

Cutting the buttonhole

Once the buttonhole is stitched, cut it open using a seam ripper, or small sharp scissors. To prevent cutting too far, place pins across each end of the opening. You may need to over sew the buttonhole edges again for a neater finish.

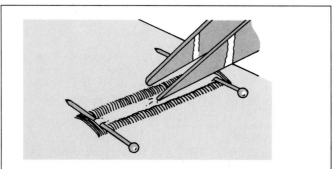

Bound Buttonholes

This type of buttonhole should be made before the garment facings are attached. There are several different methods of making bound buttonholes but some of the techniques used are common to them all.

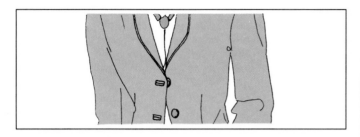

1. Mark the position of the buttonhole precisely.

2. Stitch carefully using small stitches. Do not finish with back stitches, instead pull ends to the wrong side and tie off.

3. There are two methods of slashing the opening, the first is to cut along the centre to within 5 mm (¹/₄") of of each end, then clip diagonally into the corners. The second method is useful for fabrics that fray easily. Cut from the centre diagonally into each corner. **Note:** Whichever method you use take care not to cut the stitches.

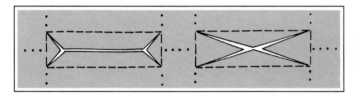

4. It is very important to secure the ends of the buttonhole to prevent them from fraying. With the right side of the garment uppermost, fold the garment back and stitch back and forth over the little triangles at each end.

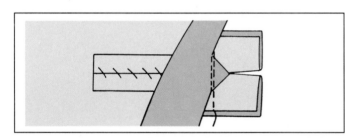

5. Lightweight interfacing can be added to reinforce the buttonholes. If the whole area does not need interfacing, cut a rectangle of interfacing 2.5 cm (1") longer and wider than the buttonhole and centre it over the markings.

6. If the interfacing is stiff, for example canvas, make the buttonhole in the fabric only. Cut holes in the interfacing the same size as the buttonholes, then apply it to the garment. Pull the back of the buttonhole through the hole to the wrong side and herringbone stitch the edges to the interfacing.

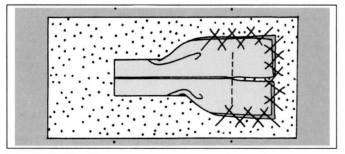

Patch Method

This simple method is ideal for light to mediumweight fabric.

1. From the garment fabric cut a patch 5 cm (2") wide and 2.5 cm (1") longer than the buttonhole.

2. With right sides together centre the patch over the button-hole markings. Machine tack/baste through the centre of the patch, along the button position line. Then machine tack/baste again 6 mm (¹/₄") either side of and parallel to this line.

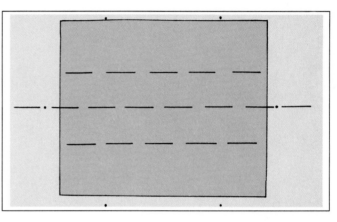

3. Fold, then press the top edge of the buttonhole patch down along the tacked/basted line. Beginning and ending exactly at the markings, use a small stitch to sew 3 mm (¹/₈") from the fold.

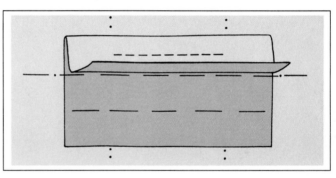

4. Fold and stitch the other lip in the same way.

5. On the wrong side check that all five lines of stitching are parallel and 3 mm (¹/₈") apart. Re-stitch any if necessary.

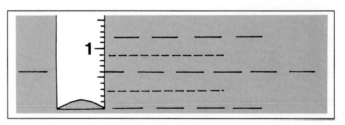

6. Remove tacking/basting stitches, then cut carefully along the centre of the patch. From wrong side slash along the centre line, between stitching, and diagonally to the corners.

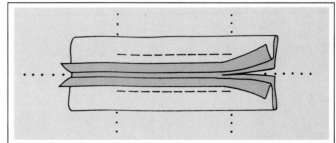

7. Push the patch through to the wrong side and tack/baste the lips together; press.

8. With the garment right side up, fold the garment back and stitch back and forth over the little triangles at each end.

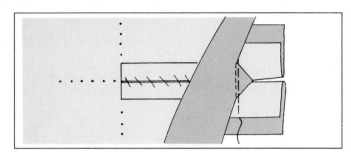

9. Trim the patch to 5 mm (¹/₄") from the stitching line.

One Piece Folded Method

This method is also suitable for light to mediumweight fabrics, but differs from the patch method because the lips are folded before they are attached.

1. Cut a piece of garment fabric 2.5 cm (1") wide and 2.5 cm (1") longer than the buttonhole.

2. With wrong sides together fold the long edges so that they meet in the centre.

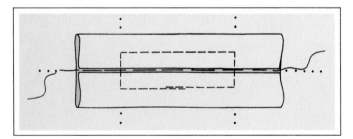

3. With the cut edges facing up, centre the patch over the buttonhole markings. Tack/baste through the centre.

4. Using small stitches, start at the centre of one lip and stitch around the buttonhole marking, working the same number of stitches across each end and pivoting at the corners.

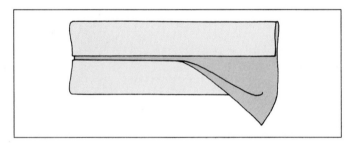

5. Remove the tacking/basting and slash through the centre of the patch and the garment, between the rows of stitching clipping diagonally into the corners.

6. Turn the patch through to the wrong side and tack/baste the lips together; press.

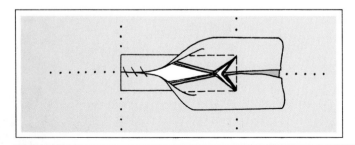

7. With the garment right side up, fold the garment back and stitch back and forth over the little triangles at each end.

8. Trim the patch to 5 mm (¹/₄") from the stitching line.

Piped Method

The addition of piping cord adds strength and stability to the edges of the buttonhole. The piping for all the buttonholes is made as a continuous strip, the length of each buttonhole plus 2.5 cm (1"), multiplied by twice the number of buttonholes (each buttonhole requires two strips). Piping cord over 3 mm (¹/₈") in diameter is not suitable for this method, because the lips would be too bulky.

1. Cut a strip of garment fabric 2.5 cm (1") wide and the required length.

2. Fold the strip over the piping cord, pin the edges together then using a zipper foot stitch close to the cord.

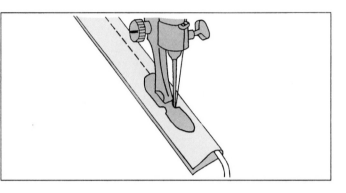

3. Cut up the strip, each piece to be the length of the buttonhole plus 2.5 cm (1").

4. Pin one strip to the right side of the garment, over the buttonhole markings, the piped edge should be 6 mm (¹/₄") from the centre line of the buttonhole; tack/baste in position.

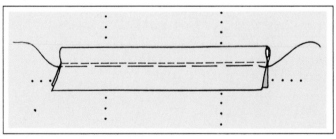

5. Using a zipper foot, small stitches and starting and finishing at markings sew the length of the buttonhole, just inside the previous stitching line. Attach the second strip in the same way.

6. Slash along the centre line, clipping diagonally into the corners.

7. Turn the strips through to the wrong side and tack/baste the lips together; press.

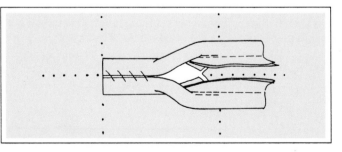

8. With the garment right side up, fold the garment back and stitch back and forth over the little triangles at each end.

9. Trim the strips to 5 mm (¹/₄") from the stitching line.

Two Piece Patch Method

This is a good method to use for fabrics that fray.

1. Cut a patch from a colour matched sheer lining fabric 2.5 cm (1") longer and wider than the buttonhole.

2. With right sides together, centre the patch over the buttonhole markings.

3. Using a small stitch and starting in the middle stitch around the buttonhole markings, pivoting at the corners and overlapping the stitches at the starting point.

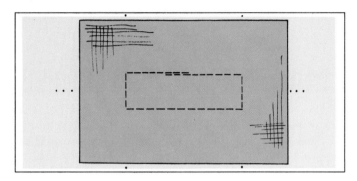

4. Slash through the centre, clipping into the corners. Turn the patch through to the wrong side, and press the seam allowances away from the opening.

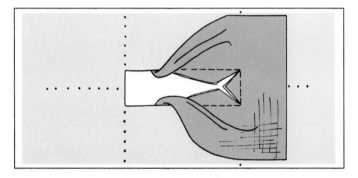

5. Cut two strips of garment fabric 2.5 cm (1") wider and longer than the buttonhole. With right sides together, tack/baste through the centre; press the seam open.

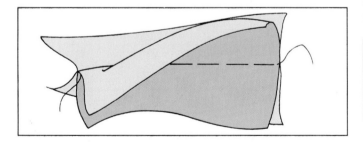

6. Place the strip accurately over the wrong side of the opening. Pin each end in place.

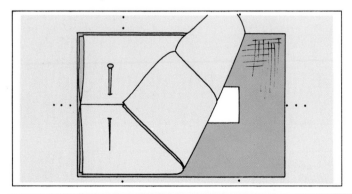

7. Turn the garment to the right side and check that the lips are even. Fold the garment back and stitch back and forth over the little triangles at each end.

8. Then stitch the lips to the garment, as close as possible to previous stitching, extending the stitching beyond the original seam.

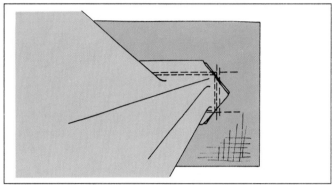

9. Trim the patch and lips and press.

Finishing Bound Buttonholes

To finish this type of buttonhole it is necessary to make an opening in the facing behind it. While the lips of the buttonhole are stitched together and working from the outside, stick a pin through each end of the buttonhole. Then on the facing side slash between the pins and turn under the raw edges to expose the buttonhole opening. Carefully slip-stich the facing in place around the buttonhole.

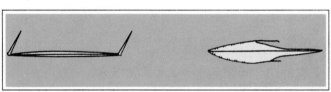

For a slightly crisper finish insert pins at each corner of the buttonhole, then on the facing side slash along the centre and clip diagonally into the corners. Turn the raw edges under and slip-stitch in place.

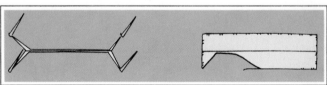

In-seam Buttonholes

These buttonholes are just openings in a seam.

XIII. Fastenings

1. Mark the position of the buttonhole, and with right sides together tack/baste the seam.

2. For each buttonhole cut two stays from a lightweight fabric 2.5 cm (1") wide and 2.5 cm (1") longer than the buttonhole. Centre the stays over the buttonhole markings, on each side of the seam, tack/baste in place.

3. Stitch the seam stopping and back-stitching at the buttonhole markings.

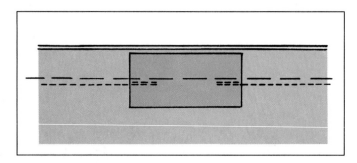

4. Press the seam open, trim the stays so that they are narrower than the seam allowance. Hand sewn bar tacks can be added to each end of the buttonhole on the wrong side for added strength.

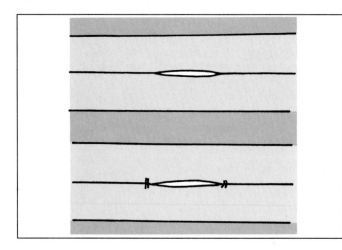

Hand Worked Buttonholes

This type of buttonhole is worked by cutting a slit through all layers of fabric and then working buttonhole stitch over the raw edges.

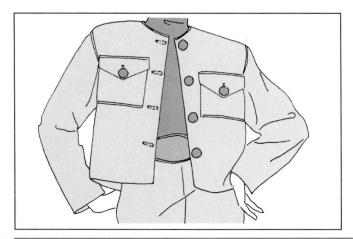

For horizontal buttonholes, the button end has fanned stitches, and a straight bar tack at the opposite end. For vertical buttonholes both ends should be finished in the same way.

1. With small stitches machine a rectangle 3 mm (1/8") around the buttonhole position line.

2. Slash along the position line, and over sew the edges.

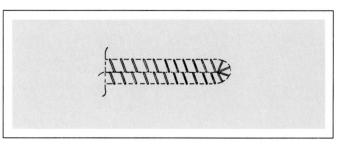

3. With the fanned end of the buttonhole to the right, fasten matching buttonhole thread to the bottom left corner, then working from left to right insert the needle through the slash to the right side just outside the line of machine stitching. Loop the thread under the point and the eye of the needle . Pull the needle to form a small knot at the cut edge, (buttonhole stitch).

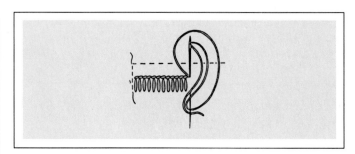

4. Working stitches close together continue along the edge, at the end fan the stitches, then turn the fabric around and work along the other edge.

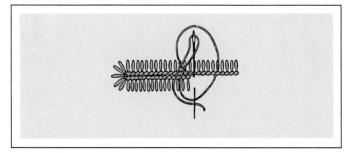

5. At the end work a bar tack of several stitches across the two rows of buttonhole stitches; fasten off.

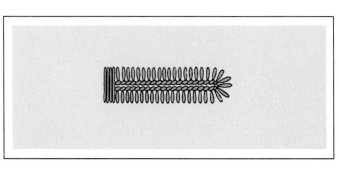

If preferred, bar tacks can be worked at each end.

Button Loops

Button or rouleau loops can be used in place of buttonholes to give a decorative finish to a garment. Style permitting, a narrow fabric tube can be set into a seam at the edge of the garment, or applied to the outside in a decorative shape. Ball type buttons are the most suitable for this type of fastening.

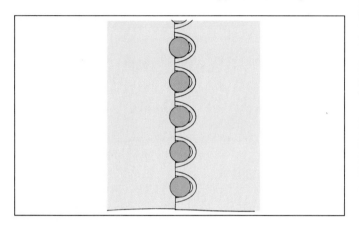

There are two methods of applying button loops, singly or in a continuous strip. The spacing between the loops and the weight of the fabric will determine the most suitable method. Small buttons are most effective placed close together, and so it is best to use the continuous method.

Fabric Tubing

A fabric tubing or rouleau is used for button loops and making decorative frogs. It is also suitable for tie fastenings, shoulder straps, spaghetti straps and belt loops.

Cord Filled Tubing

1. Cut a piece of cord twice the length of the finished tie, plus 10 cm (4").

2. With right sides together, fold the tie in half lengthwise, over the cord.

3. Sew back and forth across one end of the tie to secure the cord. Then stitch along the length being careful not to catch the cord in the stitching. A zipper foot will make this easier.

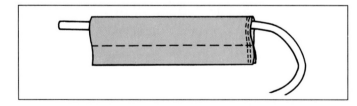

4. Trim the seam allowances, then to turn the tie the right side out, slowly pull on the enclosed cord.

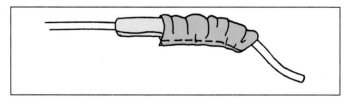

Self Filled Tubing

1. Cut the tie from the bias of the fabric the required width, plus enough seam allowance to fill the tube.

2. Fold the tie in half lengthwise with right sides together. Stretching the fabric slightly stitch along the seam.

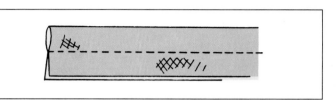

3. Thread a tapestry needle with a short length of strong thread and attach this to the end of the tube. Pass the needle through the tube, gradually turning the tubing to the right side.

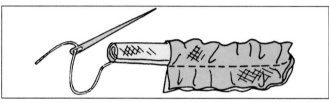

Positioning button loops

Establish the spacing and size of the loops. On a piece of lightweight paper mark the length of the opening, and the seamline. Centre a button on the seamline and lay the tubing around it. Mark the spread (the diameter of the button plus twice the thickness of the tubing). Also mark the outer edge (half the diameter of the button plus the thickness of the tubing) on the paper. Draw a line for the outer edge, parallel to the seamline and mark the positions of the remaining loops, leaving space between them if required.

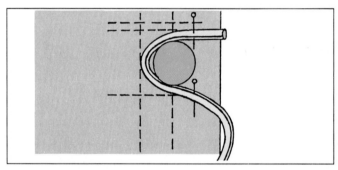

Single Loops

1. Cut individual lengths of tubing long enough to to fit within the markings, plus seam allowances at each end.

2. With the seam side uppermost, form each loop over the paper guide. Use a piece of masking tape to hold the ends of the loops in position. Machine tack/baste close to the seamline.

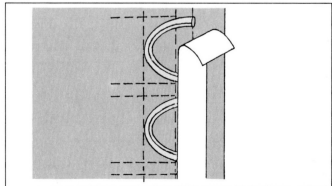

XIII. Fastenings

Continuous Loops

1. Place the continuous strip over the paper guide, turning in the seam allowance, use a piece of masking tape to hold the ends of the loops in position.
2. Machine tack/baste close to the seamline.

To reduce bulk clip the turns in the tubing after the machine tacking/basting has been done.

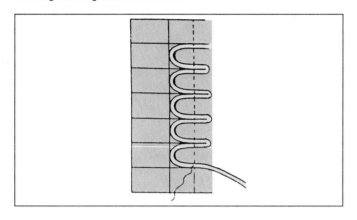

To attach loops

1. Pin the paper guide to the right side of the garment, matching seamlines, (the loops pointing away from the garment edge).
2. Carefully stitch the paper and loops to the garment along the seamline. Tear the paper away.

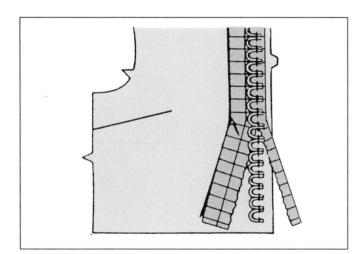

3. With right sides together pin a facing to the garment over the loops, then stitch from the garment side inside the previous lines of machine tacking/basting.

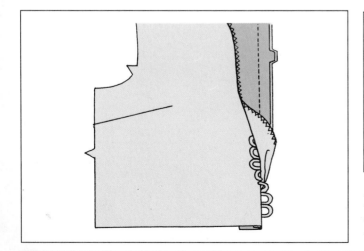

Positioning Buttons

Overlap the garment edges, matching centres, as if it were buttoned.

With a horizontal buttonhole, stick a pin through the buttonhole at the end closest to the garment edge. With a vertical buttonhole, insert the pin through the centre of the buttonhole, 3 mm (1/8") from the top. This marks the spot for sewing on your button.

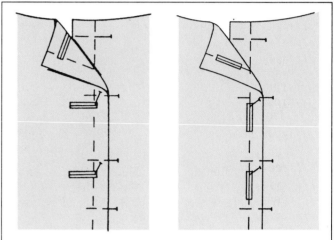

Sewing on Buttons

Buttons come in two styles, sew-through and shank. The shank is designed to compensate for the thickness of the garment. On sew-through buttons you can use thread to create a shank if required.

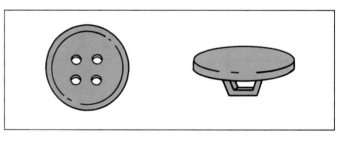

1. Thread the needle with a double thread or with buttonhole thread (a thicker thread type). Make a few backstitches to lock the thread at the position of the pin marking.
2. Bring the needle up through button and back down again and through the fabric. Repeat several times.

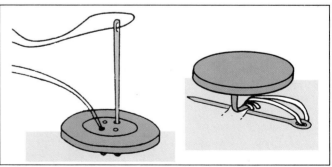

3. If the button requires a thread shank, place a match-stick or tooth-pick over the top of the button and sew over it. Remove the stick, lift the button and wind the thread round and round the extra thread between the button and the garment.

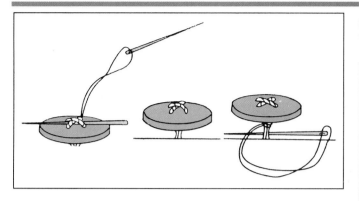

4. Bring the needle to the underside of the garment and fasten with several small tight backstitches. Insert the needle into the fabric and tunnel it between the fabric layers for about 2.5 cm (1"). Bring out the needle and cut the thread close to the fabric. On sheer fabrics cut the thread close to the backstitches.

Reinforced Buttons

This method of application is particularly suitable for suits and coats made in heavy fabrics, or in places that are under great strain.

1. Place a small flat button on the inside of the garment, directly under the garment button. Each button must have the same number of holes. A match stick or tooth pick is then placed on top of the large button.

2. Sew through from one button to the other, passing over the match stick.

3. Finish off as given for point 4 of sewing on buttons.

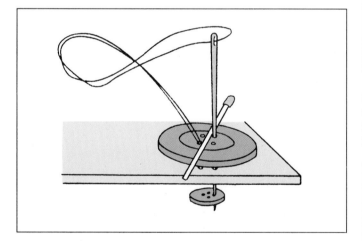

Making Buttons

Covered Buttons

For hard to match fabrics, covered buttons may be the answer. There are kits with instructions available, but it is also possible to use plastic or bone rings which are sold at haberdashery shops to make your own covered buttons.

1. Select an appropriate sized ring for the finished button and cut a circle of garment fabric a little less than twice the diameter of the ring.

2. With small running stitches, gather the edge of the fabric. Place the ring in the centre and pull up the gathering thread and secure the ends.

3. A decorative finish can be added by using buttonhole twist to backstitch through all layers close to the inside of the ring.

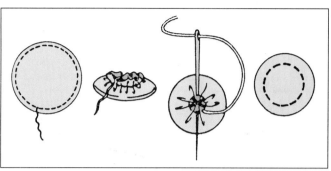

Chinese Ball Buttons

This decorative button can be made from fabric tubing or round braid and is used with frogs, (see page 85). The button should be tested first to get the correct size.

1. Secure one end of the tubing to a piece of paper. Then following the diagrams below and keeping the seam of the fabric tubing downwards loop and weave the tubing as indicated, taking care not to twist the tubing.

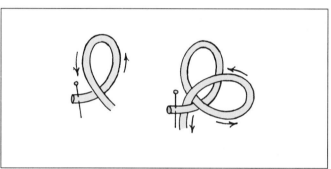

2. Pull the ends to tighten the loops and ease them into a ball shape.

3. Trim the ends and fasten them securely to the underside of the button.

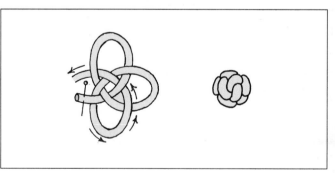

Hooks and Eyes

Hooks and eyes may be used alone or in combination with another fastening, such as a zip. They are available in a range of sizes to suit heavy to light fabrics. Hooks come with a choice of round or straight eyes - your choice depends on where you are using it. For edges that meet use a hook and round eye. For edges that lap use a hook and straight eye.

XIII. Fastenings

An important point to remember when using hooks and eyes is that your stitches should not show on the right side of the garment. Stitch them to the inside layers of fabric only.

On edges that meet

1. On the inside, sew the hook 3 mm (⅛") from the right-hand edge of the garment by whip stitching through the holes. Then sew across the end, under the curve of the hook.

2. Sew the eye opposite the hook, letting it extend slightly beyond the garment edge. Sew a few stitches across the sides of the loop to hold it flat.

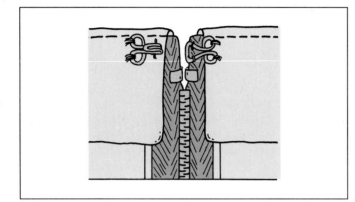

On edges that lap

1. Sew the hook to the inside of the garment on the overlap 3 mm (⅛") from the edge. Whip stitch in place, sewing through the holes and then across the end under the curve of the hook.

2. Close the zip (or whatever fastening) and mark the eye position with pins on the outside of the underlap. Sew in place.

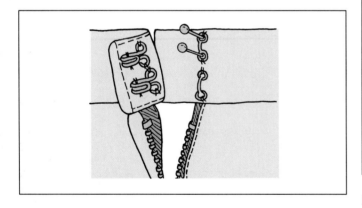

On a waistband use two sets of regular hooks and eyes or one heavy duty 'trouser' hook and bar.

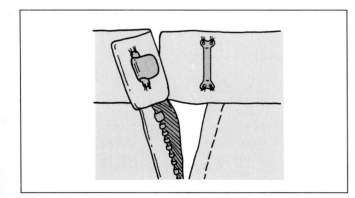

Thread Loops

Thread loops can be used in place of metal 'eyes' on fine or delicate fabrics. If made longer this method also can be used for belt carriers. The thread used should match the garment colour, to make the loop as inconspicuous as possible.

Blanket Stitch Loops

1. Attach the thread securely to the garment. Then on the right side make 2 or 3 stitches the required length. Secure with back-stitches.

2. Work closely spaced blanket stitches over the strands of thread, fasten off securely.

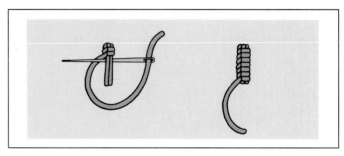

Thread Chain Loops

1. Attach the thread securely to the garment. Make a loop, by taking a small stitch. Hold the needle and thread end in your right hand. With the thumb and index finger of your left hand hold the loop open.

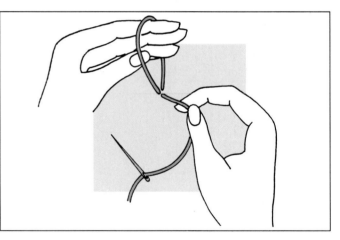

2. With the middle finger of your left hand, pick up the thread attached to the needle and draw it through the loop.

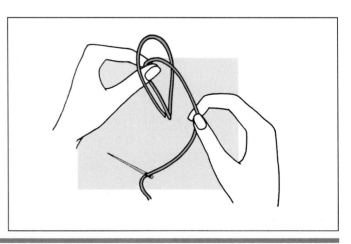

3. Allow the loop to slip off your thumb and index finger, towards the fabric, so that it tightens.

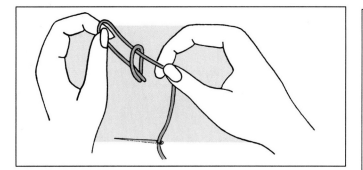

4. Continue until the chain is the required length, then pass the needle and thread through the loop, to secure the chain.

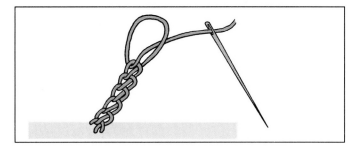

5. Fasten the free end to the garment.

Frogs

These are decorative two-part fasteners, that can either be commercially bought or made in the following way. The opening edges of the garment can either be lapped or meet edge to edge. The ball or button side should be on the left side for women.

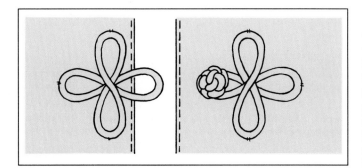

To make frogs

1. Draw the frog design on a piece of paper.
2. Following the diagram below pin a piece of fabric tubing (keeping the seam uppermost) or round braid to the paper.

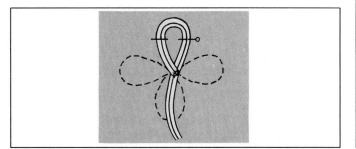

3. Whip stitch where the tubing crosses, taking care not to let ends or stitches show on the right side. Remove the paper.

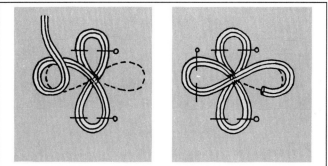

4. Make a second frog in the same way.

To attach frogs

1. Close the garment (lapped or edge to edge, according to the design) and place the frog face up with the button loop over the opening edge, slip-stitch or whip stitch in place from the under side. Attach the second frog to the other edge at the button position. Sew on a ball or Chinese button, (see page 83).

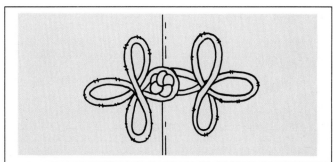

Press Studs or Snaps

Press studs are used on edges that overlap which are not under strain.

Sew the ball half to the inside of the garment on the overlap, positioning it approximately 3 mm ($^1/8$") from the edge. Whip stitch several times through each hole. To keep the stitches from showing on the outside, pick up only two or three threads of fabric with each stitch and tunnel the needle between the layers of fabric as you go from hole to hole.

To mark the corresponding socket position, close the garment and stick a pin through the centre of the ball to the underlap.

Sew the socket half in place in the same way as the ball half.

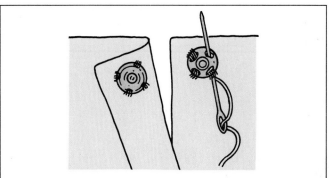

XIII. Fastenings

No-sew Fastenings

Some snap fastenings and 'trouser' hooks and eyes do not require sewing. They can just be hammered into position. Special tools are sometimes required and are generally on sale in kit form alongside, or with, the fasteners.

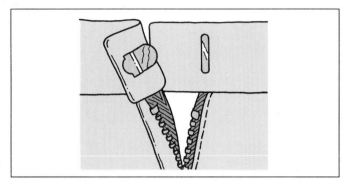

Zips or Zippers

This type of fastener is a lot easier to insert than you may think. There are many types of fasteners and the one you choose will depend on the style of your garment.

Check your pattern envelope for the length and type of zip to buy. Some garments, such as jackets, may require an open-ended or separating zip. Consider also the weight of the zip in relation to the weight of your garment fabric. For example, a flexible lightweight synthetic zip will be better suited to a dress in a lightweight fabric than a less flexible heavyweight metal zip.

In order to understand the instructions for inserting a zip, first make yourself familiar with the parts of it.

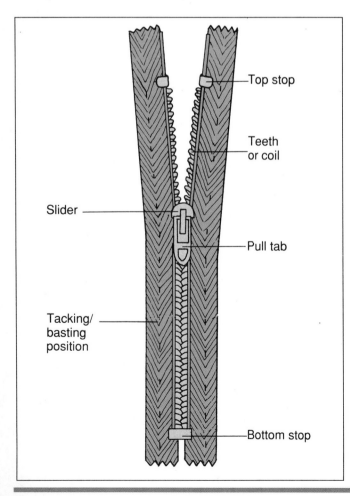

- Top stop
- Teeth or coil
- Slider
- Pull tab
- Tacking/ basting position
- Bottom stop

Shortening a zip

If the zip length required is not available it is always better to buy a longer one and shorten it. Measure the desired length then create a new bottom stop, by whip stitching 8 to 10 times across the teeth or coil. Cut off the excess zip and tape.

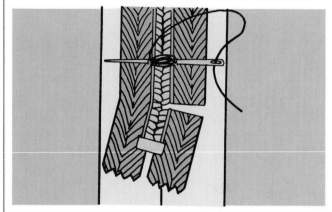

Open-ended or separating zips can only be shortened from the top.

Position the zip so that the excess length is at the top edge where it will be encased by a waistband, collar or facing. Cut off the surplus zip, level with the raw edges.

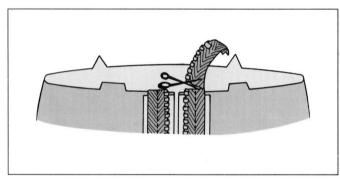

Inserting a zip

1. Close the zip and iron out any folds, but do not iron over synthetic teeth.

2. Stay-stitch the edges of the fabric opening before inserting the zip particularly if there is a risk of stretching - on knits or bias seams for example.

3. Always pin and sew your zip in one direction to prevent distortion.

4. A zipper foot is essential for machine stitching. Straight stitch machines often have a zipper foot which slides from left to right so that you can stitch with the needle on either side.

5. Adhesive tape is an effective aid to positioning the zip prior to hand tacking/basting and stitching.

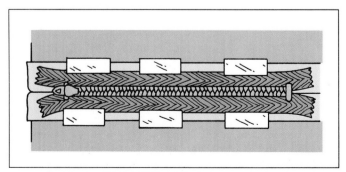

Centred Zips

This method of zip insertion is used at the centre back or front of garments with conventional zips.

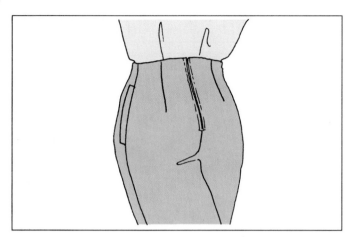

1. Mark the length of the zip, then stitch the remainder of the seam to this point, back-stitching at the end.

2. Tack/baste the remainder of the seam. Press open and finish the raw edges.

3. On the wrong side, centre the closed zip face down over the seam allowances. Tack/baste in position.

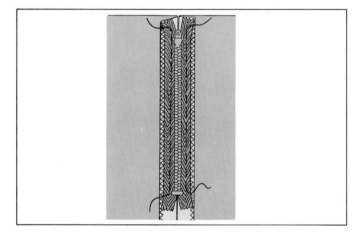

4. On the right side, starting at the bottom of the zip, top-stitch across the bottom of the zip, then up one side, close to the tacking/basting stitches, and through all the layers.

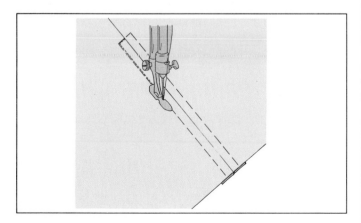

5. Stitch the second side in the same way, starting from the bottom.

6. Remove the tacking/basting stitches.

Lapped Zip

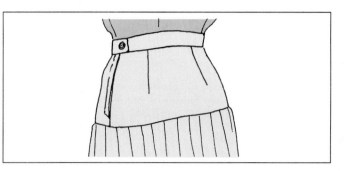

1. Mark the length of the zip, then stitch the remainder of the seam to this point, back-stitching at the end.

2. Tack/baste the remainder of the seam. Press open and finish the raw edges.

3. Turn to the inside, extending the right-hand seam allowance, position the zip face down, centred over the seam.

4. Tack/baste in place along the right-hand seam allowance.

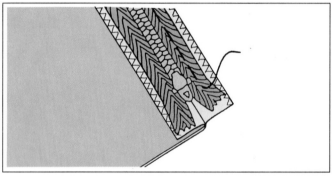

5. Turn the zip face up, making a fold in the seam allowance, close to the zip teeth. Then stitching through all thicknesses sew along the folded edge.

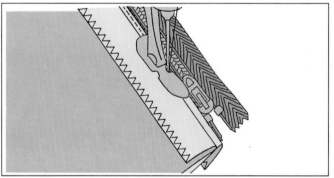

6. Turn the garment to the right side and tack/baste the zipper tape to the garment, then starting at bottom top-stitch across the end and along the side of the zip, pivot at the corner.

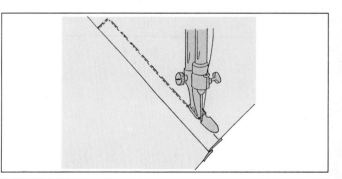

XIII. Fastenings

Open-ended or Separating Zip

For the best results insert open ended zips before facings are attached and hems are sewn.

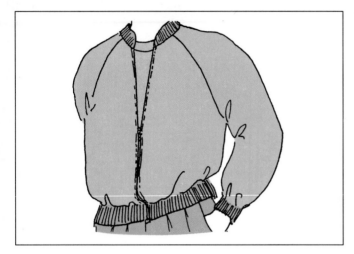

1. Tack/baste the opening edges together, and press open.

2. Centre the closed zip face down on the seam allowances, with the bottom stop and bottom of the garment level. Tack/baste in place.

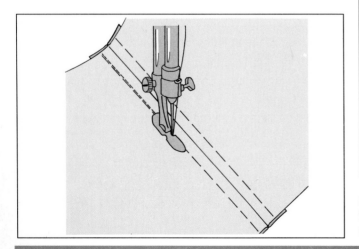

3. On the right side of garment top-stitch along each side of the zip, parallel to the centre seam. Pull the ends through to the wrong side and tie.

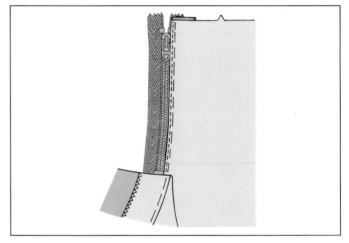

Fly Front Zip

This type of zip application is traditionally used for men's trousers, but has become popular on womenswear. The method below is a simplified version and the placket crosses from right to left not left to right.

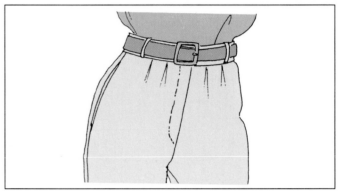

1. Mark the length of the zip, then stitch the remainder of the seam to this point, back-stitching at the end.

2. Fold both extensions to inside along foldlines, and tack/baste close to the edges.

3. Place the closed zip under the left front, the teeth close to the folded edge, tack/baste in place, then stitch.

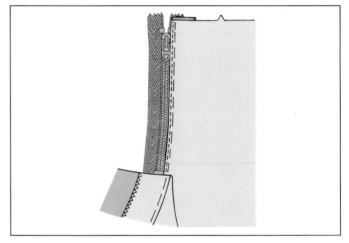

4. Matching centre front markings, lap the right-hand edge over the zip and tack/baste through all thicknesses close to the fold.

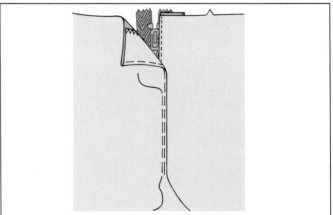

5. From the inside tack/baste the zip along the stitching line, through all layers.

6. On the outside of the right front top-stitch, through all layers

along the tacked/basted markings. Pull all threads to the wrong side and tie.

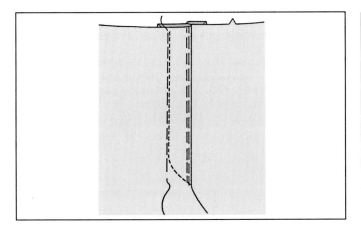

Exposed Zip

This type of zip application is used when there is no seam.

1. From matching lining, cut a patch 7.5 cm (3") wide and 5 cm (2") longer than the zip. Mark the length of the opening on the centre of the garment.

2. With right sides together tack/baste the patch in place along the centre line.

3. Stitch 3 mm (1/8") on each side of the centre line and across the bottom of the zip marking. Slash along centre line to within 5 mm (1/4") of end and clip diagonally into the corners.

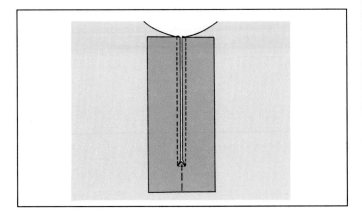

4. Turn the patch to the inside and press. With the zip bottom stop at the end, centre the zip under the opening, tack/baste in place.

5. With garment right side up, fold the garment back and stitch back and forth over the little triangle at the end.

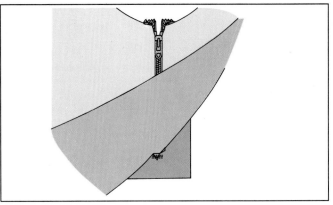

6. Then turn back one edge, and starting at the bottom, stitch the zip tape to the garment and patch seam allowances along the first stitching line. Stitch the other side in the same way.

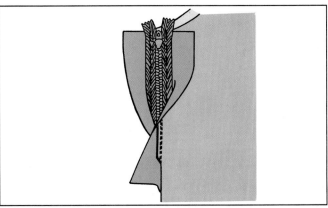

Concealed Zips

Concealed or invisible zips differ from standard zips in application and appearance. When closed only the pull tab is visible from from the outside of the garment. They require a special zipper foot, and are applied to open edges prior to the seam being stitched.

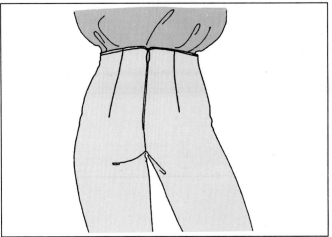

1. Finish the edges that the zip is to be applied to if required.

2. On the right side of the garment place the open zip face down. With the teeth lining up with the seamline, pin the tape to the seam allowance.

3. Fit the right-hand groove of the zip foot over the teeth and stitch from the top edge to pull tab.

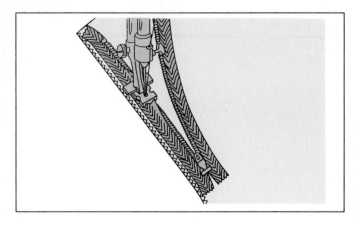

4. Close the zip and then pin the unstitched tape to the other seam allowance. Open the zip and fit the left-hand groove of the zip foot over the teeth; stitch from the top edge to pull tab.

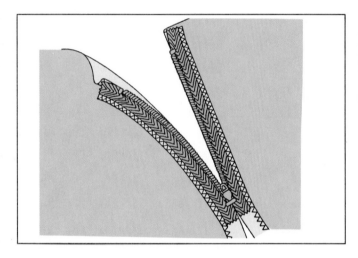

5. Close the zip and pin the seam allowances together below the zip. Using a conventional zipper foot to the left of the needle, lower the needle into the fabric to the left and slightly above the last stitch; sew seam.

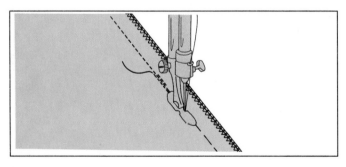

6. To hold the tapes in place, stitch them to the seam allowances.

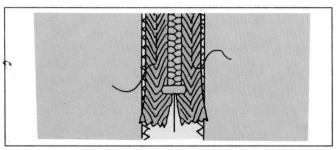

Tailoring Touches

Shoulder Pads

Shoulder pads are often an integral part of a garment's fashion silhouette. In addition to enhancing the fashion look, shoulder pads can be a quick and easy way to improve the fit of a garment.

Narrow or Hollow Shoulders

Shoulder pads can fill the natural hollow that occurs just below the shoulder. They can also add width to narrow shoulders.

Uneven Shoulders

This is a common fitting problem that is easily corrected with different sized shoulder pads. The shoulder that is lower gets the thicker pad. Do not try to get away with just one pad for the lower shoulder. The result will be bumpy and lop-sided.

Large Busts

Try adding small shoulder pads to your garments. By adding balance to the upper body, shoulder pads can minimise the appearance of a large bust.

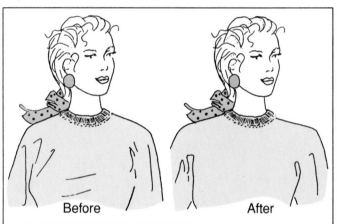

Before   After

Choosing shoulder pads

Shoulder pads are available in the traditional style for set-in sleeves, as well as in extended shoulder styles for kimono, raglan sleeves or drop shoulders. The set-in sleeve pad has a defined edge, the extended style is curved over the shoulder.

The type of garment you are making determines the size and type of pad you will need.

Use 5 mm to 1.5 cm (1/4" to 1/2") thick pads for blouses and dresses. This size is occasionally used for jackets when a small pad is required.

Use 1.5 to 2.5 cm (1/2" to 1") thick pads for jackets and coats. This size is occasionally used for dresses when an over-sized look is the fashion focus.

Attaching the shoulder pad

On set-in sleeves

1. Pin the shoulder pad to the inside of the garment so that the largest layer of the pad is against the garment. The shoulder line of the pad should match the shoulder seam of the garment and the straightest edge of the pad should extend 1.5 cm (1/2") beyond the armhole seam.

2. Try the garment on to check the pad placement.

3. Remove the garment then loosely hand sew the pad in place to the shoulder seam allowance and along the armhole seam allowance.

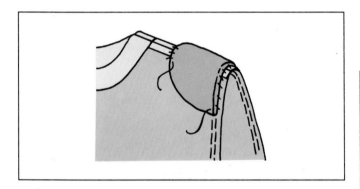

On kimono, raglan or drop shoulders

1. Try on the garment. Slip the pad inside and position over the shoulder. Pin in place from the outside of the garment.

2. Remove the garment and loosely stitch the underside of the pad to the shoulder seam allowance.

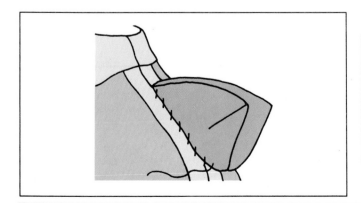

Removable shoulder pads

Velcro fasteners are a convenient means of attaching shoulder pads, enabling you to take them in and out and use the one set on a number of garments - such as sweaters.

Attach the hook side of the Velcro to the shoulder pad (this means it will also hook on to knitwear if required) and the loop side to the garment.

Shoulder Pad Covers

Sometimes, particularly in the case of unlined jackets and coats, you will want your shoulder pads to be in the same fabric as your garment. These covers are easy to make for unshaped pads.

1. Cut a rectangle of either lining or garment fabric big enough to cover both sides of the pad, plus 1.5 cm (1/2") all round.

2. Position the shoulder pad so that the straight edge of the pad is on the bias of the covering fabric.

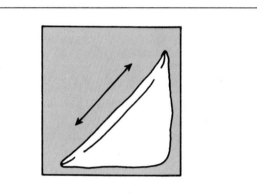

3. Fold the lining/fabric over the pad.

4. Straight stitch along the edge of the pad, trim the seam allowances to 5 mm (1/4") and zig-zag over the raw edges.

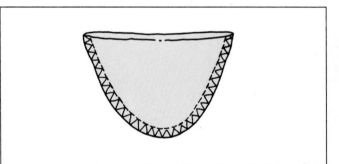

XIV. Tailoring Touches

Lining

Linings not only enhance the finished appearance of a garment, but are functional in hiding the seams and raw edges on the inside. This is particularly necessary for jackets and coats. The lining used will depend on the type of garment - jacket and coat linings should be strong to withstand wear and tear, whereas a dress lining should be lighter in weight. Also jackets and coats could benefit from the added warmth of a thicker lining.

The method of application also varies with the design of the garment. For skirts and trousers the lining can be free hanging, attached to the garment at the waistline. This type of lining can be added to most skirts or trousers, whether the pattern includes lining pattern pieces or not. The lining is cut out using the garment pattern piece. If a skirt is pleated the pleats are folded on the pattern piece before cutting the lining. For jackets and coats the pieces can be joined by machine and then sewn in by hand or machine. Separate pattern pieces are required for this type of lining.

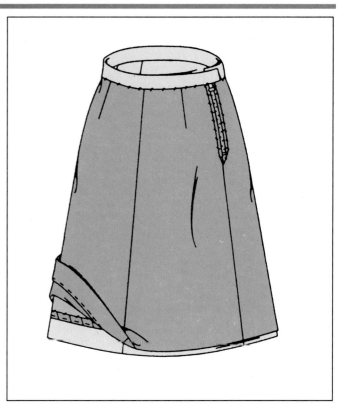

Free Hanging Lining

1. Cut the lining out using the garment pattern pieces.

2. Make up the garment, including inserting zips and finishing hems.

3. Stitch together the lining pieces and press the seams open. If the garment has a zip opening leave this part of the seam open on the lining.

4. Turn the garment inside out and with the wrong sides together pin the lining to the garment. Pin the lining opening around the zip opening, then slip-stitch in place.

Lining a Jacket by Machine

1. Complete the garment section, apart from securing the facings to the shoulders.

2. Stay-stitch along the outer curved edges of lining, then join all the pieces together. Machine tack/baste across the top and bottom of the centre back pleat.

5. Tack/baste the lining to the garment at the waistline, then attach the waistband.

6. Turn up a hem on the lining 2.5 cm (1") shorter than the garment hem.

3. With right sides together, pin then tack/baste the lining to the facing matching the shoulder seams. With the lining side uppermost and starting at the centre back, stitch to twice the depth of the hem from the lower edge. Stitch the other side in the same way.

4. Trim, grade and notch the seam, then press the seam

allowances towards the lining.

5. Turn to the right side, and lifting up the garment fabric **loosely** hand sew the lining to the garment along the underarm seams. Hem the sleeves and lower edge of the lining.

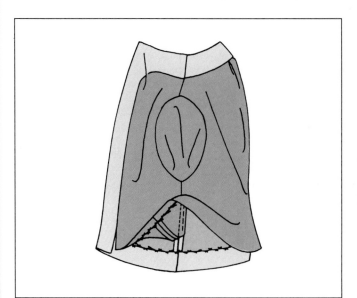

Index

Index

PRINTED IN BELGIUM BY

proost

INTERNATIONAL BOOK PRODUCTION